Needlework
in
America

Needlework
in
America

History, Designs, and Techniques

Virginia Churchill Bath

A Studio Book

The Viking Press
New York

Text and black-and-white photographs
Copyright © Virginia Churchill Bath 1979
All rights reserved
First published in 1979 by
The Viking Press/A Studio Book
625 Madison Avenue, New York, N.Y. 10022
Published simultaneously in Canada by
Penguin Books Canada Limited

Library of Congress Cataloging in Publication Data
Bath, Virginia Churchill.
Needlework in America.
(A Studio book)
Bibliography.
Includes index.
1. Needlework—United States.
I. Title.
TT751.B3
746.4'0973   79–1488
ISBN 0–670–50575–7

The drawings and photographs of needlework
techniques are by V. C. Bath
Text and black-and-white photographs
printed in the United States of America by
The Murray Printing Company, Westford, Massachusetts
Color photographs printed in Japan by
Dai Nippon Printing Co. Ltd., Tokyo

Designed by Michael Shroyer

Jacket designed by Christopher Holme

For
Verda and James Churchill
and for the Baths: Russell G., Russell C.,
Kenneth, Sylvia, Beverly, Alec, Michele,
Jamey, and Casey

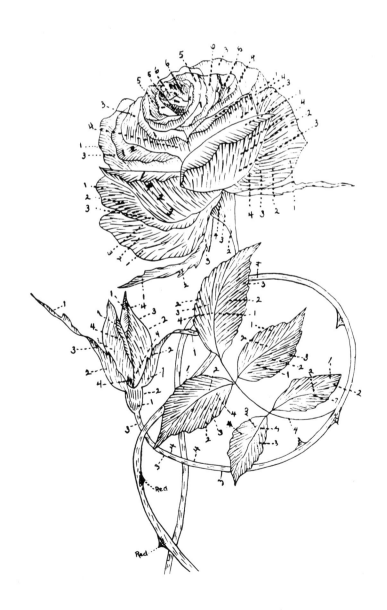

Also by Virginia Churchill Bath

Lace

Embroidery Masterworks

Contents

Acknowledgments

I wish to thank the following people who helped in assembling the photographs for this book: Christa Mayer Thurman, curator of textiles, and Howard Kraywinkel, John Mahtesian, and Linda Cohn of the Photography Department, Art Institute of Chicago; Barry A. Greenlaw, curator, and Prim Specht, Bayou Bend Collection, Museum of Fine Arts, Houston; Ron Testa, photographer, Field Museum of Natural History, Chicago; Jean Mailey, curator, and Barbara Teague, Textile Study Room, The Metropolitan Museum of Art, New York; Larry Salmon, curator of textiles, and Elaine Zetes, Photography Department, Museum of Fine Arts, Boston; Nora Fisher, curator of textiles, and Arthur Olivas, photographic archivist, The Museum of International Folk Art of the Museum of New Mexico, Santa Fe; Elizabeth S. Winton, director, Old Gaol Museum, York, Maine; Elsie McGarvey, curator of costumes and textiles, Philadelphia Museum of Art. Thanks are also due to Alice Postell, business manager–curator, Sheldon Jackson Museum, Sitka, Alaska; J. Herbert Callister, curator of textiles and costumes, and Abbie F. Hodges, manager of the Atheneum Shop of The Wadsworth Atheneum, Hartford; Karol A. Schmiegel, assistant registrar, The Henry Francis du Pont Winterthur Museum, Winterthur, Delaware; Sanna Deutsch, registrar, Honolulu Academy of Arts; Ruth Morrissey, curator, and Otto Thieme, research associate, Helen Louise Allen Textile Collection, University of Wisconsin, Madison; Lockett Ford Ballard, Jr., director, Litchfield Historical Society, Litchfield, Connecticut; Joan Severa, curator of decorative arts, State Historical Society of Wisconsin, Madison; Pat LaLand, staff writer, Press Bureau, and Mildred Lanier, curator of textiles, Colonial Williamsburg; Robert G. Wheeler, vice president, collections and presentations, Greenfield Village and Henry Ford Museum, Dearborn, Michigan; and Jane C. Nylander, curator, ceramics and textiles, Old Sturbridge Village, Massachusetts.

I am grateful to those who have allowed artworks from their collections to be reproduced: Mrs. Gregg Ring (Betty Ring), Houston, Texas; Dr. Murray C. Brown, Chicago, Illinois (acting for his daughter, Kim Brown McIlhenny); Rhea Goodman, New York; and Julie Silber, San Rafael, California. Mrs. Ring and Dr. Brown were especially helpful in supplying information concerning their well-researched textiles.

Dot Woodsome, Sally Monson, and Ruth Rees suggested sources or loaned material used in the sections on techniques. Ruth Harris alerted me to certain materials at the University of Wisconsin.

A number of curators and other museum personnel were particularly generous with their time and assistance. J. Herbert Callister, Nora Fisher, and Joan Severa mounted artworks for photography especially for this book. Otto Thieme and Lockett Ford Ballard, Jr., made photographs themselves. Larry Salmon spent time searching out and showing me textiles that had not been published previously.

Finally, I want to thank Russell G. Bath.

Sampler made by Anne Gower.
Essex Institute, Salem,
Massachusetts.

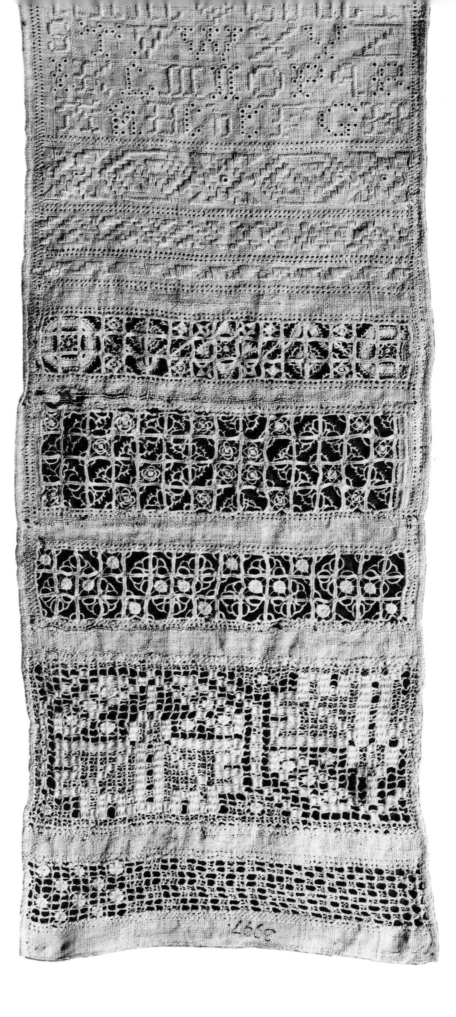

Introduction

The oldest sampler in the United States was made in England about 1610 by Anne Gower, later the wife of Governor John Endecott. This sampler and a half-dozen others made before 1700 conjure up pictures of young women leaving for the New World, their carefully worked embroideries stowed for the voyage.

Settlement of America began in earnest in the early seventeenth century. By 1620, the year when thirty-two wives joined their husbands on the *Mayflower* for the voyage to Plymouth, many other wives and prospective brides already had made the voyage to Virginia.

The first attempts at colonization in Virginia, which eventually became the model British colony, had been faltering and painful, but by 1612 prospects had brightened. Women were beginning to arrive, and experiments with raising and curing tobacco had shown it to be the money crop of the future.

In 1622 there were 1,240 inhabitants in the colony. That year a savage Indian massacre wiped out a third of the population and all its budding industries, among them several associated with textiles: the breeding of silkworms and the making of silk, the production of flax and hemp, and the manufacture of glass beads. After the massacre the settlers who remained devoted themselves almost exclusively to raising tobacco.

In 1619 a Dutch ship had left part of its cargo of slaves from Africa in America. Slaves offered a cheaper and steadier source of labor than indentured workmen. The planter who could organize a series of endeavors and keep them going could now more easily grow rich. The wisest masters diversified into shipping, warehousing, brickmaking, and other cash-producing industries.

The grandeur of the Virginia plantation house is legendary; the first of these baronial households dates from 1642 when Sir William Berkeley arrived in Jamestown to take up his duties as governor. His mansion, Green Spring, was built two miles from town. Stocked with superb English furnishings, silver, and books, it set the standard for great houses to come.

Life on a plantation was an isolated existence, and socializing was a necessity. Greenhouses, bowling greens, deer parks, and even racetracks provided diversion.

Despite all this wealth and leisure, there is, curiously, little evidence of needlework by Southern ladies. In contrast, many examples made by women of the Northern colonies exist. Possibly the plantation masters, reflecting the classic Greek attitude, believed that the work of artists and craftsmen—and all who worked with their hands—represented a secondary level of endeavor.

There are, of course, other probable reasons for the lack of Southern needlework. The climate undoubtedly was a factor. In the North, needlework was produced methodically and in a disciplined fashion, as part of a structured school curriculum, but most Southern children were instructed on the plantation.

The formal nature of Southern household furnishings, and the prevalence of professionally made imported objects, may have discouraged amateurs. Although Southern needleworks are scarce, those known to have been made on the plantations are exquisite. No coverlets were more subtly designed or more carefully quilted than those associated with Westover-Berkeley, Hillsborough, and Mount Vernon.

Life in New England was, of course, quite different. Massachusetts Bay Colony early made itself as independent as possible of England. Despite the vast numbers of religious refugees of various sects who made their way to the New World, it was only those who came to Massachusetts Bay who undertook to establish a colony based on the laws of their religion. Huguenots, Roman Catholics, Quakers, Moravians, Mennonites, mystics, Pietists, and Jews came from England, France, and Central Europe because they were unable to worship as they wished in their homelands, but only the Puritans created their own commonwealth, based upon the order and discipline dictated by their religion. Twenty thousand people came to Massachusetts Bay Colony in the first twelve years.

The colony was closed to people of other religions, and art, music, and literature were inspected as possible sources of corruption that might be impediments to God's purpose. In 1634 an edict of the General Court of Massachusetts forbade the wearing or owning of clothing with lace of any type, thread (linen) lace as well as gold or silver. Slashed garments (those with decorative cuts through which an undergarment, often embroidered or lace trimmed, could be seen) as well as clothing with embroidery or cutwork also were on the list of garments subject to confiscation.

The moralistic view of matters of dress is reflected in lines from "Against Pride in Clothes" by The Reverend Isaac Watts, which appeared in a collection of his works published in 1720:

How proud we are! how fond to shew
Our clothes! and call them rich and new!
When the poor sheep and silk worms wore
That very clothing long before.

The tulip and the butterfly
Appear in gayer coats than I,
Let me be drest fine as I will,
Flies, worms, and flowers exceed me still.

Then will I set my heart to find
Inward adornings of the mind;
Knowledge and virtue, truth and grace,
These are the robes of richest dress.

The records of the Massachusetts Probate Court reveal that some houses in the colony were fashionably furnished before the eighteenth century. However, their appointments included few paintings; instead, there were more likely to be mezzotints, and engravings, which sometimes served as models for embroidery.

Little seventeenth-century household embroidery remains, but documents give evidence of the kind of needlework that was in use. An inventory of the estate of Governor Theophilus Eaton, made in New Haven in 1656, lists "canvis and Turkey work." In the same year the inventory of Anne Hibbins of Watertown, Massachusetts, contained a "wrought cupboard cloth." In 1660 she listed "six needlework cushions and four drawn to work." These were valued at ten pounds, a high price. In 1687 Samuel Sewall, the Massachusetts jurist and diarist, ordered from England fustian bed hangings and chair covers marked with designs for embroidery. Samplers and embroidered pictures do not appear in the probate records until 1700, but after 1750 the frequency of their mention indicates that, apparently, many were made.

It is not always possible, of course, to be sure whether a needlework listed in an inventory is of American or English origin. Many pieces were imported from England; others were made according to English patterns and using English fabric. Determining where Turkey work was made has proved one of the most challenging enigmas. Twenty-five years ago a number of existing pieces worked in this technique were thought to be of American origin; more recent research indicates that they are probably English.

The New England farmhouse offered a welcome contrast to the often inhospitable climate; it was a colorful, cheery place. It might contain Windsor chairs, rural versions of Chippendale or Queen Anne furniture, and chests or other pieces gaily painted or carved. Silver, pewter, brass, pottery, and engravings contributed to the effect of warmth. Color was added with needleworked or pattern-woven cushions, table covers, and bed furnishings. Chip carvings, samplers, documents, and emblems also provided spots of interest, to say nothing of the drying herbs and skeins of bright freshly dyed yarn hanging from the rafters.

Among the earliest New England colonists were experienced carpenters, and at an early date expertly constructed houses showing current subtleties of design began to appear.

Later there also were buildings that, like the brick architecture of Williamsburg, reflected the style of Georgian England. Adam and classic revival styles were chosen for Charleston's wide-verandahed houses, and in New Orleans a French Creole innovation, the lacy ironwork balcony, was added. Spanish styles appeared in the Southeast.

The French built houses with logs set vertically. They plastered the walls, frescoed the ceilings, and even eventually installed well-finished hardwood floors. These houses were furnished with imported French articles and handsome Indian items.

It was the Swedes along the Delaware who, in the eighteenth century, introduced the first cabins with horizontally set logs. Their style was well suited to the frontier, and it moved westward with the German, Scottish, and Irish builders. At first, round logs were chinked with mud or clay, but later the logs were squared, dovetailed at the corners to fit snugly, and mortised and pinned. Oiled deerskin paper was used at the windows.

The first of these log houses were built in Pennsylvania, which was very different from both Virginia and New England. Pennsylvania was, from the beginning, a melting pot of nationalities and religions. The Protestant Quakers were not welcome amid the Puritans of New England. The beliefs that had caused them to be persecuted in England also set them apart in the New World. William Penn became interested in the Quaker religion as a college student, and despite the concern of his father, Admiral Sir William Penn, he continued in his beliefs. When Admiral Penn died, William agreed to take payment of a debt of £16,000 from Charles II in the form of land in the colonies, in order to establish a haven for the Quakers. In March 1681 the king gave William Penn a charter granting him the right to govern a large region west of the Delaware River.

In 1681 there were a thousand settlers in Pennsylvania, Germans among them. Penn came the following year with a hundred more, and in the same year he bought Delaware from the Duke of York in order to be sure of having access to the sea. Philadelphia was laid out in 1682.

When Penn's emigrants came to America, they did not arrive in wilderness. Development along the rivers of Pennsylvania already had given the area a distinctive heritage that produced art unlike that of New England. The Delaware River was discovered by Hudson in 1609; in 1616 it was explored by the Dutch, who acquired rights to shorelands in 1623. In 1627 Swedish and Finnish colonists settled on the west bank of the Delaware (Zuydt) and the Hoarkill. Between 1638 and 1659 other Swedes settled in the valleys of the Schuylkill and the Delaware. The English came into the Schuylkill valley in 1641 and in 1653 drove out the Swedish settlers. The seat of government, established in 1643 at the site of Philadelphia, changed hands several times. In 1655 the Dutch took it from the Swedes; in 1664 the English took possession; and in 1672 the Dutch regained the territory. In 1681 the Dutch ceded the colony to England, and in 1682 Penn took possession. Before the turn of the century Penn had anglicized names, and many new English colonists had arrived. German Township, an area given to German emigrants, attracted many nationalities. By mid-century it was the most fashionable suburb of Philadelphia.

The area also saw the arrival of Swiss Mennonites and the Amish, who joined the other settlers between 1708 and 1720 in what was to become Lancaster County. They were to figure prominently in the history of American needlework. In the second and third quarters of the eighteenth century three hundred and eighteen shiploads of German, Swiss, Dutch, French, Danish, and Swedish emigrants came to settle in Pennsylvania. The Moravians, who were to produce exquisite silk embroideries in their schools, arrived in this period, too. The newcomers included well-educated men and skilled craftsmen.

Fractur, or *Fraktur*, was a type of design used by itinerant craftsmen in making birth and marriage certificates, and also for other documents, house blessings, and valentines. The term comes from sixteenth-century Latin lettering used in Germany in which the characters are thin and have pointed ends and serifs. The earliest book on fractur published in America, *Deutsche und Englische Vorschriften für die Jugend,* was printed by Carl F. Egelmann in his shop near Reading. His book included designs of angels and cherubim of Swedish style and designs taken from English porcelain. Some of his patterns appealed to embroiderers.

The community of Ephrata was founded in 1732 by Conrad Beissel, an apprentice weaver from Germantown. The designs that he made for his music books are closely related to those found in source books used by weavers. Among his widely reproduced patterns, one of the most familiar was the Holy Mystic Lily, which was not confined to the Pennsylvania area, but also appeared on Bible boxes and chests made in Connecticut. This motif also was used for embroidery.

A lace manufacturer and printer from the Netherlands named Reynier Jensen arrived in Pennsylvania in 1697. Five years before emigrating to America, Jensen had decided to go into the lace business, but in the New World he returned to printing and was in charge of the colony's Quaker press. It is thought that Jensen's interest in lace was significant in the development of Pennsylvania design. Many Pennsylvania German patterns are close to those found in books of design for cutworks and lacemaking. Italian, French, and English pattern books all seem to have been influences. The lily and rose of Sharon of Pennsylvania crafts are seldom found on Rhineland chests, but they do appear on chests made in Pennsylvania, Connecticut, and Massachusetts.

Early Pennsylvania German households had few ornamented textiles; their houses were decorated with carvings and painted designs. Their craftsmen were so proficient in these arts that at first they seem to have eclipsed embroidery and weaving, but after a time young girls began making needlework for their dowries. Show towels with thread-counted stitches and drawnwork were made to cover the utilitarian towel on the wall rack. Samplers were stitched with crewel. The patterns of Hesse, the Palatinate, Alsace, and Switzerland were remembered. One finds the Tree of Life, flowers, peacocks, and other birds (sometimes in confronting pairs), star forms (which were at times intended to represent the pomegranate), cocks, pelicans, unicorns, lions, double-headed eagles, fish, and mermaids. Sometimes these motifs were used with their original symbolic meanings in mind; more often they appear to be purely decorative.

In the long day of most colonial housewives many hours were devoted to textile production. In wealthy establishments there were weaving houses where many hands, black ones among them, labored

Plate 1. Octopus bag. Sheldon Jackson Museum. Photograph by Alice Postell.

Plate 2 (left). Bed rug made by Philena McCall, Lebanon, Connecticut. Wadsworth Atheneum, AMDEC Fund.

Plate 3 (below). Embroidered hearth rug made by Jane Naomi Strong, 1829. Wadsworth Atheneum, gift of Miss Mary Todd.

Plate 4. Bed rug made by Hannah Johnson (1770–1818) and dated 1796. Art Institute of Chicago, gift of the Needlework and Textile Guild.

Plate 5. Detail of an early
eighteenth-century valance.
Woolen embroidery on linen. Art
Institute of Chicago, gift of Mrs.
Albert H. Barber.

Plate 6 (right). *Cymbeline*. The composition is derived from a stipple engraving by Thomas Burke. An inscription on the mat which surrounds this needlework reveals that it was "Wrought by Ann Trask at Mrs. Rowson's Academy." Silk embroidery on silk, with heavily painted details. Old Sturbridge Village.

Plate 8 (below). Sampler made by Hannah Carlile, 1796. Silk on linen. The style of embroidery in this and the sampler opposite is associated with Miss Polly Balch's school. Collection of Mrs. Gregg Ring.

Plate 7 (above). Memorial picture, probably derived from an engraving by Enoch Gridley or a painting by John Coles, Jr. Collection of Mrs. Gregg Ring.

Plate 9. Sampler made by Lucy Potter, 1791. Providence, Rhode Island. Art Institute of Chicago, gift of Miss Naomi Donnelley through the Needlework and Textile Guild.

Plate 10 (above). Footstool cover
in Berlin wool work, 1860–80. Helen
Louise Allen Textile Collection,
University of Wisconsin. Photograph
by Otto Thieme.

Plate 11 (left). Sampler in
Philadelphia style. The inscription
is partially picked out, but the date,
1820, is still distinguishable.
Collection of Mrs. Gregg Ring.

Plate 12. Sampler made by Mary Antrim of Burlington County, New Jersey, in 1807. Collection of Mrs. Gregg Ring.

Plate 13. Appliqué portiere (1901)
designed by George Washington
Maher (1867–1926) and Louis J.
Millet (1853–1923). Art Institute
of Chicago, gift of the Antiquarian
Society.

Plate 14. Small beadwork bag with woolen embroidery, satin lining, and ribbon drawstrings. 1860–80. Courtesy Helen Louise Allen Textile Collection, University of Wisconsin. Photograph by Otto Thieme.

Plate 15 (right). Anna Tuel's marriage quilt. Wool, linen, and cotton patches with calamanco border, unbleached wool interlining, and lining of plaid blanketing. Courtesy Wadsworth Atheneum, gift of William L. Warren in Memory of Florence Paull Berger.

Plate 16 (below). Framed Medallion (detail). Pieced, appliquéd, and embroidered quilt made by Jane Warwick in 1795. Collection of Mrs. John B. McIlhenny, on loan to the Art Institute of Chicago.

Plate 18 (right). Hawaiian quilt made before 1918. Honolulu Academy of Arts.

Plate 19 (below). Detail of a Baltimore quilt. Metropolitan Museum of Art, Sansbury-Mills Fund, 1974.

Plate 20 (left). Quilt in Star of Bethlehem pattern with eight Le Moyne Stars made by Miss Submit Gay. Awarded a silver medal by the Hartford County Agricultural Society in 1842. Wadsworth Atheneum, gift of Miss Fanny Gay Darrow.

Plate 21 (below). Central medallion quilt with stars and pinwheels, ca. 1845. Courtesy Joel and Kate Kopp, America Hurrah, New York City.

Plate 22. Coverlet (detail). Silk
crazy-quilt blocks with elaborate
compound embroidery stitches.
1884. Art Institute of Chicago, gift
of Miss Helen Donathen.

in the preparation of linens and clothing, but for most families the flax brake and scutching board for linen preparation; the shears, washtubs, combs, and cards for wool preparation; the hackle, the spinning wheels, the niddy noddy, the reel, the dye pot, the swift, the bobbin winder, the scarne, the warping frame, and the loom were personally used household equipment. All these tools, with the possible exception of the flax brake, the scutching board, and sheep shears, were used by women.

Yarn dyeing was a project for the winter months, but all year round women collected berries, barks, and leaves to try out as dyes. They learned much from Indian women. Although they made a great variety of shades, at first only the blues from indigo were washfast, and dyeing with indigo was a long, disagreeable process. Eventually, women learned how other colors could be mordanted to make them permanent.

The early mordants were kitchen staples such as soda, cream of tartar, salt, vinegar, or lye. Drip lye could be made from wood ashes, and chamber lye (urine) also was used. Sumac and oak provided mordants. Alum and copperas (ferrous sulfate) had to be purchased. Blue vitriol (copper sulfate) and chrome (potassium dichromate) also were useful. The pot in which the dyeing was done could affect the color of the textile. Brass pots were used for bright colors, iron ones for dark shades.

The colonists recognized sumac, which they had used at home, as an excellent dye plant. It is said that Governor Endecott introduced woodwax (*Genista tinctoria*) as a dye in Massachusetts, but it also was found in Maine by Henry Josselyn. Also called dyer's greenwood or woadwaxen, it is used with woad or indigo to make green. Browns, grays, tans, yellows, rusts, and orange were the colors for which dye materials were easiest to find, but there was also a demand for reds, blues other than indigo, and purples. Blacks were made from poison ivy or mercury; they were difficult to mordant effectively. Iris and elderberry gave lavender shades, but they were fugitive.

Books on dyeing began to appear in America in 1798. Recipes for the use of brazilwood as a red dye for cotton or linen were eagerly tried. In 1815 a book by Evert Duyckinck and Elijah Bemiss, *In Conformity with an Act of the Encouragement of Learning,* listed twenty recipes for making lavender, the most-coveted color, with logwood and brazilwood or peachwood. For women without this book there was still the possibility that the purple paper wrapped around the sugar that came from the West Indies might yield a good dye if soaked.

The list of dye recipes is endless. The beauty of natural colors, like the quality of hand-spun yarn, has led contemporary textile people to investigate old procedures. Home dyeing declined after 1857, when the first of William Henry Perkin's aniline dyes were produced.

The designs that colonial women used depended to a great extent upon where they lived. Along the coast, English patterns and excellent imported materials were available. Inland, designs were acquired from a local artist, a peddler, or made by the woman herself. Because most of the settlers were English, most early needlework reflects English design. It has been said that because materials were expensive or because they had to be made at home, there was a tendency to use stitches that put most of the thread on the surface of the work and to make open, widely spaced designs, but the fact that wealthy women also used these stitches suggests that the ease and rapidity with which they could be worked also may have been a factor.

On the plantations of the South, where there was no shortage of help and where the masters spent lavishly to create showplaces, prodigious projects were undertaken. Large pieces of matched white cloth were used for quilt grounds. Special English chintzes were purchased for appliqué. Embroidery was made with silk thread.

By the fateful year of 1776 there were five hundred thousand black Africans in America. The women among them learned textile crafts early. Their practiced fingers could pick the seeds out of cotton to be used to fill a quilt more deftly than would Eli Whitney's machine later in the century.

When it came time to decide upon a style for the new capital city for the United States, Thomas Jefferson recommended the "good Roman manner" of Christopher Wren. The appetite for the classical manner had begun with the excavations at Herculaneum in 1738. England's regency, France's empire, and America's federal style were similar, all classical.

Some of the classical motifs of England's Robert Adam (1728–92) that found their way into embroidery were translated also into American design by Salem's Samuel McIntire (1757–1811), an architect and furniture maker, but above all, an expert carver. Adam's bellflower swags, husks, and fans and McIntire's eagles, wheat sheaves, cornucopias, and flower baskets were perfect motifs for embroidery design.

The late eighteenth century was the heyday of the classic colonnade, but since mid-century a Gothic revival had slowly been gaining momentum. In time this resulted in the castles of stone—or painted imitations of stone—mansard roofed and metal columned, that appeared in many American cities and along the Hudson River. Copies of picturesque details from buildings of Switzerland, Venice, and the Near East were cast in iron or cut with a scroll saw. In these mansions furnished with souvenirs of a Grand Tour, there was little space for adornments made by loving hands at home.

The houses of Andrew Jackson Downing (1815–52) had already begun a trend that would lead to a new style more hospitable to domestic embroidery. Downing was an architect and the landscapist of the Capitol, the White House, and the Smithsonian Institution. He was the first American writer to adopt the idea that nature and architecture should be compatible, an idea later exquisitely developed by Frank Lloyd Wright. Downing deplored the Greek fad. (In 1846 he said that he was relieved that the "Greek temple disease has passed its crisis.") Downing was an early exponent of function-following form, but as it turned out, all his favorite influences were highly ornamental or romantic. He liked the colors of nature; he liked English cottages, log cabins, Swiss chalets, and French and Italian farmhouses; he also liked the currently fashionable battlements and turrets and the decorations of the Moors and Orientals. These predilections combined to inspire large, comfortable, verandahed and turreted houses embellished with scrolling wooden lacework, oriel windows, stained glass, and dripstones.

The Downing version of cottage architecture was by no means intimate and cozy. While their half-timbering, leaded windows, and earth colors gave his buildings a look of rusticity, they were in fact palatial. Still, they were a change from the earlier, more formal Gothic revival designs, and they did open the way for a simpler cottage style in the English tradition. By the 1880s and 1890s the shingle style, comfortable and practical, had emerged. With its development, exotic imported needlework no longer was *de rigueur*. The setting again was perfect for well-designed domestic needlework.

These were the decades when architects turned to nostalgia and nature, and when women reflected the trend in their bright wool-embroidered cushions and tea cozies, their thread-counted versions of Caucasian rugs, and their numerous odd, collagelike needlework-paper craft projects.

Philadelphia's Centennial Exposition of 1876 introduced many Americans to the innovative work of the English designers Charles Lock Eastlake (1836–1906) and William Morris (1834–96), and to the handsome simplicity of the furniture of the Shakers. In contrast, they also encountered the exotic artifacts of the Near and Far East, which excited interest in teakwood carving, pierced metal, inlays, and especially, Oriental carpets. Soon afterward the Moorish look was fashionable. Rooms dimly lighted by the dappled color of stained glass shimmered with silken cushions, richly embroidered, and the mother-of-pearl of inlaid tables. The Turkish corner, an effort at a harem effect, was a fad calling for damascened spears, exotic feathers, and fur rugs. Clearly, it was a time for artistic reform.

American embroiderers who attended the exposition were greatly impressed by work shown by the Royal School of Art Needlework, an endeavor of the South Kensington Museum (now the Victoria and Albert Museum). English embroidery designers had for some time been engaged in a conscious campaign to improve their art. William Morris had begun to make designs for embroidery as early as 1855, preparing elaborate projects for needlewomen working directly under his supervision, and kits for customers to embroider. The kits contained not only designs by Morris, his daughter May, or J. H. Dearle, his chief assistant, but also fabrics and threads woven and dyed at his Merton Abbey workshops. Americans purchased many products of the workshop, so many that in the October 3, 1888, issue of *The World* George Bernard Shaw lamented that May Morris exhibited at the first Arts and Crafts Exhibition only her "quieter achievement, all her great curtains covered with fruit-forests having presumably been ravished across the ocean by millionaire fanciers of the States." Walter Crane and Sir Edward Burne-Jones also were leaders of design. Late English examples showed Arabian, Turkish, or Persian influences.

Art Needlework was espoused in England by noblewomen, churchmen, and architects in an effort to promote needlework that was excellent in design and more refined than Berlin work. They founded the Royal School of Art Needlework in 1872. They were not concerned with educating—or reeducating—the middle class (although they planned to use the services of talented and relatively needy women to do the embroidery), but middle-class women soon took up the new designs and materials. Much less of their work remains than of Berlin wool work; Art Needlework was fragile and succumbed to use. Large pieces and church work are the main survivors. Mantelpiece borders (lambrequins), heavy portieres and curtains were typical ambitious projects. Clothing was decorated, and many small pieces of household linen were embroidered.

At a mundane level Art Needlework usually involved earthy, dull colors, probably in reaction to the vivid tonal clashes of Berlin work. Much of the embroidery was done in Kensington stitch, a version of stem stitch. Medievalism prevailed; many designs were Jacobean in origin. Flowers, as always, were popular, but they were stylized, rather than sentimentalized. Small wildflowers were favored. Parrots were replaced by cranes. Japanese mannerisms were copied. Scrolling and various Renaissance grotesqueries made an appearance.

Berlin work had peaked in America about 1856 but continued to be popular until about 1886. However, among those influenced by the Art Needlework shown at the Philadelphia Centennial was Candace Wheeler, a gifted designer of printed linens and woven silks for Cheney Brothers. She was to become a major force in the efforts to move American needlework away from the standardized, sentimentalized designs of Berlin wool work. Her book, *The Development of Embroidery in America,* is a classic on the subject. While most of her designs were stitched by others, she herself worked some of the rich silk and velvet designs—an example is a portiere now in the Metropolitan Museum of Art. Dating from about 1884, it is made of silk and embroidered in silk, with a plush border; it shows the influences of both Oriental embroidery and the designs of William Morris.

Another important figure in the modernization of embroidery was Louis Comfort Tiffany (1848–1933). A member of a famous Massachusetts family of goldsmiths and a founder of the Society of American Artists, Tiffany was a leader in the *art nouveau* style that followed the Arts and Crafts movement of Morris and his associates. (In England and Scotland *art nouveau* took a less fluid and more rectilinear form known as the Glasgow style.) Like many of his contemporaries, Tiffany was attracted to Byzantine design. His workshop produced glass, metalwork, jewelry, wallpapers, murals, tapestries, and books. Vestiges of Tiffany stylization can be found in the humblest patterns for cushions and doilies of the period.

In New York, Tiffany, Candace Wheeler, and others formed the Society for Decorative Arts in an effort to organize needlework and other women's crafts on a business basis. As in England, where schools and needlework societies were formed in many places, schools were started in many American cities. Embroideries in the modern style were produced at the Roycroft School, established in Aurora, New York, in 1895, and also at Pratt Institute in New York City. Classes were offered by the Guild of Needle and Bobbin

Portiere designed by Candace Wheeler. Nineteenth century. Metropolitan Museum of Art, gift of the family of Mrs. Candace Wheeler, 1928 (through Mrs. Boudinot Keith).

Crafts, an affiliate of the prestigious Needle and Bobbin Club, whose bulletins are invaluable to those interested in historical needlework. In Chicago, the Needlework and Textile Guild was organized at the Art Institute of Chicago.

The Deerfield Blue and White Society, the Colcha Club of New Mexico, and the lacemaking revival at Ipswich led by Mabel Foster Bainbridge are a few of the later efforts to continue techniques and preserve embroideries of the past.

But the important development in embroidery at the turn of the century was expressed by Lewis F. Day in *Art in Needlework*, written in 1900: "Design was once upon a time traditional; but the chain of tradition has snapped, and now conscious design must be eclectic—that is to say, one must study old work to see what has been done, and how it has been done, and then do one's own in one's own way. It is at least as foolish to break quite away from what has been done as to tether yourself to it. And in what has been done you will see, not only what is worth doing, but what is not."

For a brief period in the early twentieth century the passion for coordinated decorative arts and the wealth of clientele combined to give the United States something resembling a needlework profession. In the November 1917 issue of *American Architect*, in an article on "Laces and Their Affiliation with Architecture," William Laurel Harris showed lace patterns made to echo the design of paneling and windows. One wonders how many sets of curtains would have had to be made to last through the life of the carving!

An example of the care with which architects coordinated details of decoration is seen in the portiere (Plate 13) designed for the James A. Patten house in Evanston, Illinois, built in 1901. George Washington Maher was the architect, and the portiere was designed in collaboration with Louis J. Millet, a decorative artist. A thistle motif was used throughout the house; the portiere, which is made of cotton and silk fabric in cut-velvet weave, has a thistle pattern in damask-woven cotton appliquéd with machine embroidery and silk cording. The stylization and almost two-dimensional simplicity of the design make it a fitting opener for twentieth-century needlework. A static quality allies it with the Glasgow school rather than with *art nouveau*, and its kinship with early ecclesiastical appliqués on velvet links it with the past.

Maher worked primarily in the Middle West. Some of his residences and public buildings, like those of Louis Sullivan and Frank Lloyd Wright, were geometrically simple, with dominant arches. Others, like his own residence in Kenilworth, Illinois, were intricately romantic, with octagonal porches and bays, leaded windows, and steeply sloped roofs. His interiors were richly paneled, carved, and painted, and the furniture carving, sometimes heavily Gothic, exactly matched the architectural carving.

The Arts and Crafts movement, which had started in America in 1876, was ending by the time Harris wrote his article for *American Architect*. The introduction of the sewing machine, shortly before the Civil War, had brought an end to wide-scale hand sewing. In fact, it started the exodus of women from the home.

The most surprising thing about the needlework of the past is how seldom it has emanated entirely from the imagination of the maker. One of the encouraging facts about the needlework of the last few years is that not only the artists who have been drawn to it but also the hobbyists are seeing the virtue of making their own designs. The Embroiderers' Guild and National Standards Council of American Embroiderers and other groups now are full of members who are constantly improving in their understanding of how to design for embroidery. It may be that the major contribution of the twentieth century to the art of embroidery is the idea that needlework profits when designer and maker are the same person.

Many of the needleworks illustrated in this book are masterpieces that have been familiar for a long time; other fine works are being published for the first time. Some of the textiles were selected because they represent an unusual technique. With space limited, only a few articles made in the twentieth century could be included. Also, a number of needleworks that would have added greatly to this collection were, for one reason or another, unavailable.

People who do needlework are constantly on the lookout for new patterns; therefore, drawings that can be put to this use have been included. The directions for stitches and processes may also be helpful. Some techniques of the past no longer are widely known; it is hoped that readers may come across new ideas among these old needleworks.

I North American Indian Needlework

Woman's robe with ribbon appliqué.
Fox. Field Museum of Natural
History.

North American Indian Needlework

North American Indians excelled in various arts, depending upon their mode of life. Architecture, weaving, silverworking, and pottery making naturally developed most among sedentary agricultural tribes, while hunters and nomads were more apt to be superior in carving, textile ornamentation, and other decorative techniques.

Three strains of influence are apparent in Indian design. Consistent with the theory of the migration of ancient Asians across the Bering Strait, northern Indian art seems to have Oriental roots. Other tribes, living in mid-continent, created designs that shared characteristics with those of the Indians of Central and South America. Ideas absorbed from the European arts of the colonists are apparent in the work of the Indians of the eastern seaboard.

Designs migrated with the Indians. For example, the floral style, considered to be of European origin, spread westward. The naturalistic botanical patterns of the Cree and Chippewa (Ojibwa) made their way into the arts of the northern plains Blackfoot, the Nez Percé, and the plateau tribes. A more stylized version of the botanical theme was developed by the Potawatomi, Sac and Fox (Sauk and Fox), and other tribes.

Indian artists were open to new motifs and materials and used them in subtle combination. Despite the many similarities, patterns never were copied exactly. Foreign ideas were welcomed. The Sioux, for example, apparently were very fond of the Caucasian rugs of their white neighbors and adapted motifs from them into their own designs. Distinctive indigenous styles were diluted more rapidly in the Southeast, presumably because of greater exposure there to European influence. Elsewhere the Indians assimilated what they liked, but retained their own idiom.

Although the colonists were quick to adopt many Indian methods of dyeing yarn, they do not seem to have picked up design ideas so readily. However, some evidence of Indian motifs can be found in quilt patterns. Indian art really did not come into its own as an important influence until the twentieth century. The geometric designs of the Navajo, Zuñi, and Hopi were the basis of

Moccasins. Quillwork on buckskin. Old Iroquois. Field Museum of Natural History.

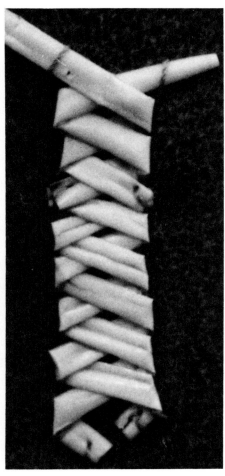

Quillwork.

some art deco patterns, and in "Of Tradition and Esthetics" (*American Indian Art: Form and Tradition,* p. 23) Martin Friedman reminds us that Frank Lloyd Wright also made use of them.

Usually embroidery, quilling, and beadwork were done by women. Some learned the arts from their mothers; others had the additional advantage of formal instruction. Among the Plains tribes, in which beading was highly developed, crafts guilds accepted the membership of only the most skilled artisans. Indians were sensitive to fine craftsmanship and recognized the individual characteristics of talented artists.

The Indian artist created within the guidelines of function and symbolism transmitted by his or her forebears. It was not the intention of the artist to express an individual state of mind. Most Indians learned and practiced the crafts, but certain gifted persons enjoyed professional stature, although usually they also had some other form of employment.

Quillwork

For most northeast woodland Indians their life style was dictated by seasonal quests for food and supplies. In the spring they tapped maple trees; in the summer they farmed, gathered wild food, and fished; in the fall they cut wild rice; and in the winter they hunted. Theirs was a semi-nomadic life, and consequently their arts were small and portable, utilizing materials they found around them—notably birchbark, skins, and quills.

Quillwork, thought to be unique to North American Indians, is an ancient art, practiced extensively, especially among nomadic tribes. Quillwork designs were used to decorate articles made of birchbark, skin, and cloth. Shirts, moccasins, dresses, gloves, knife sheaths, medicine bags, pouches, boxes, and pipe stems were among the personal articles for which quillwork was used. It also can be found in tepee decoration and on musical instruments and ritual utensils. White men living in the wilderness learned from the Indians that skin garments were practical. They had their skin clothing made according to European patterns, and sometimes the quillwork decorating them reflected foreign taste. Later, quillwork items were made especially for trade with Europeans: cardcases, spectacle cases, and small boxes.

The introduction of European glass and porcelain beads brought about a decline in quillwork, and the art had almost disappeared until recently, when a general interest in traditional crafts brought it new attention.

Eastern Algonkian ornamental
quillworked bag. Field Museum of
Natural History.

Tlingit dance leggings. Quillwork on leather with puffin beaks. Field Museum of Natural History.

To make quillwork, quills were taken from porcupines or were made from the spines of bird feathers. Porcupines live in the northeastern quarter of the United States, in the West (except in the extreme southern part), and also in Canada and Alaska. Their quills are ⅟₁₆ to ⅛ inch in diameter, naturally white with black tips, barbed, and 1 to 5 inches in length. For use in quillwork, they were soaked either in a bowl of water or in the mouth. If they were to be used flat, they were pulled between the teeth or pressed with a bone flattener. The tips were cut off.

Sometimes natural-colored quills were used. In the Great Lakes area leather was smoked dark brown or dyed black to contrast with naturally white quills. Quills take dye well. Before the introduction of commercial dyes, black and orange were the favorite colors. Indians had various ways of dyeing quills. They might put them in a vat with highly colored trade cloth and boil them. Or they might obtain dyes from plants and minerals. Reds came from the root of *Galium tinctorum* (dye bedstraw), buffalo berry, squaw currant, dock root, tamarack bark, spruce cones, sumac berries, bloodroot, and hemlock bark. Black was made from alder bark, wild grapes, hickory, walnuts, and butternut bark. Sometimes, when black was wanted, Plains Indians used the stems of maidenhair fern instead of quills. Yellow came from *Evernia vulpina,* or wolfsbane, and from wild sunflower, coneflower, black willow roots, or sumac root. Purple was made from blueberries, blue from larkspur. Greens were made with two dye baths, blue and yellow. The pithy interior of bird-feather spines took the dye especially well, so these often were used for this difficult color. Not all tribes, of course, used all the colors. Once aniline dyes were available, Indians used them.

When the quills of birds were used, they were split. Bird quills are readily identified by their ragged edges. The Cheyenne used grasses or cornhusks in place of quills, but the husks are dull in comparison to quills. On the west coast a tule grass was used for similar work.

There were many different methods of attaching quills to skin, cloth, or birchbark, all variations of the four main methods: wrapping, sewing, braiding, and weaving. Wrapping was simply a matter of closely winding the quills on a small article, such as a pipe stem. Skill was needed to work the quill ends deftly into the winding as one quill followed another into the work. Patterns could be arranged by using quills of various colors.

Sewing methods involved one line of stitching or two. The stitching was done with sinew when the work was applied to skin. In order to preserve its flexibility, the sinew was kept damp except

Vest. Quillwork on leather with
cloth binding. Missouri Historical
Society. Photograph by the author.

for the tip, which was twisted into a tight point to serve as a needle. A hole was made in the skin with an awl, and the sinew was put through it. Since the holes did not entirely penetrate the skin, the back of the work showed no evidence of the decoration on the front. Thread was used on cloth.

In one type of work a single line of running or back stitches was made, and the quill was twisted around each stitch, producing a cordlike effect. In other work two rows of stitches were made parallel to each other. If one line of quills was inserted, the effect was a close zigzag. If two lines of quills were used, one starting from each side, a braidlike effect could be achieved, as the quills crossed each other, passing in alternate directions.

Separate braids could be made by stretching two threads or strips of sinew taut in a bow, then passing the quills back and forth, over and under the pair of bowstrings.

When quills were woven, a special bowlike loom or frame was used. Warps were strung on the loom, and as wefts were woven into them, quills were laid alongside the warps.

Birchbark, a versatile material used to form the peak of the tepee, also became a background for quillwork. Birchbark containers were made by steaming the bark and sewing it with spruce roots or basswood bark. Boxes and other articles made for trade were embellished with appliqué, dental pictographs (designs incised with the teeth), or quillwork.

In decorating birchbark, short quills dyed in various colors were thrust through holes in the bark. The quill ends were bent under, and later the article was lined. The quills were kept in place by the tightness of the holes and the lining.

In the Northeast, from the Atlantic to the Ohio valley, early quillwork had simple goemetric designs; later designs were curvilinear, double curved, and based on plant forms. Narrow lines made with one-thread stitching were used for scrolls and spirals along with other motifs made of wider bands stitched with two threads. Quilled birchbark articles were made by the Ottawa, Ojibwa (Great Lakes), Micmac (New Brunswick), and Penobscot (Maine) tribes. Geometric and floral designs were used, and in the Great Lakes region naturalistic animals and birds were worked. In addition to quills, dyed moose hairs, which were about the same length as quills, were incorporated into the work. They were pushed in from the back and clipped to the desired length. Moose hairs are found most often in naturalistic floral work. Some of the designs were derived from trade goods.

One thread, one quill.

Two threads, one quill.

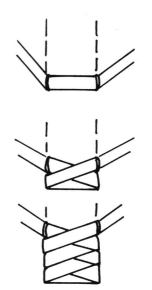

Two threads, two quills.

In the late eighteenth century the Ojibwa made a particular type of quillwork design worked on birchbark covered with black cloth. Broadcloth was used at first; later it was replaced by linen. Small articles made for trade were handled in this way, with the edges covered with bundles of sweet grass held in place by couching. In this work, on boxes, spectacle cases, book covers, and similar small items, quills were worked in imitation of European embroidery in satin, stem, and knot stitches. The designs were floral, rendered in natural pastel shades.

Indians of the northern and central plains used quillwork on skin and cloth primarily. Although there were porcupines in the southern plains, quillwork was not made in that area; weaving and embroidery were the local arts.

The Plains Indians, who were hunters and nomads, used buffalo, deer, elk, bear, and beaver skins to make clothing, shelter, and other necessities of life. North and central Plains Indian designs were angular, worked in broad bands. The oldest designs are entirely geometric. Later, a rather rigid, stylized floral design developed, thought by some to have been inspired by designs of the French. In this work single narrow lines of quilling were worked into tight coils.

Plains Indians wrapped the upper portions of fringes with quills and used braided quills on their pipe stems. The Blackfoot and Crow made large quilled disks for use on tepees or clothing. They flattened their quills only slightly, while Indians of the central plains preferred the quills quite flat. The Plains quillwork most prized by other tribes was that of the Mandan-Hidatsa.

Canadian and Alaskan Indians were no less expert than Plains workers. The densely settled northwest coast was a great center of artistic creativity. The finest quillworks, on the whole, were made above the northernmost tier of the United States.

Porcupine quills.

Notes on technique

Quills are an appealing material for needlework, unusual because they are stiff, rather than limp or wiry, as threads are. When moistened, quills are easy to work with. Their only drawback is their short length. This is of no consequence in making quilled boxes, in which the quills are used in small pieces, but it is troublesome in some other techniques.

The technique used to make boxes and other articles already has been described. Strictly speaking, it is not needlework, but a closely allied craft. The designs on these quillworks are precise and geometric. The box lids, usually round or oval, inspired com-

Sioux moccasins. Doeskin
decorated with red, yellow, and
purple porcupine quills, colored
beads in lazy stitch, and feathers.
Nineteenth century. Art Institute
of Chicago, gift of Mrs. J. Ogden
Armour.

Box cover of birchbark with
quillwork. Eastern Woodland. Field
Museum of Natural History.

positions with circles, as well as the usual triangles and lozenges. On these pieces, quills, left in their natural round state, glow softly.

In making quillwork stripes and bands directly on clothing, or to be applied to clothing, the quills, as mentioned before, often are flattened. This in no way diminishes the fine texture of the material, which imparts a pearly sheen when worked over an area. The various folded techniques using one or two lines of stitching are reminiscent of the work in gold plate that was done in Europe. Plate is a flat strip of thin metal that is applied to embroidery in exactly the same way that the Indians applied quills, except that, mercifully, the metal strips are quite long. Usually, Europeans covered the folded edges with a small gold cord, couched in place, and it was customary to work the plate over padding, in order to make it glitter more.

Any material that can be cut into strips can be used in this way. Raffia could serve as a substitute for quills, but it is not, as the photograph shows, altogether satisfactory. It is naturally uneven and soft, and it defies precise workmanship. Reeds and grasses are more difficult to handle and tend to break.

Anyone fortunate enough to have access to a supply of quills will find them interesting material. Those pictured here were purchased from an unusual food store in a Chicago suburb. They cost ten cents apiece, making quillwork a very expensive craft. A contemporary writer, discussing the problem of obtaining quills, says that road kills are the best source, but we are reluctant to suggest this potentially hazardous means.

Designs done with raffia in quillwork technique.

Beadwork

Beadwork—usually done by women, but occasionally by men—seems to have begun in the East about 1675 and about 1800 in the western territories, Canada, and the northern United States. Southeastern Indians, Indians of the southern plains, and southwestern Indians did little beading, but there are exceptions. The splendid baby carriers of the Kiowa of the southern plains are examples.

The Algonkian (New England) word for wampum was *wampumpeak* or *wampompeag*. *Wamp* means to be white, and *umpe* or *ompe* means a string of small beads. Nowadays we think of wampum as the white or purple shell beads of the Iroquois (who were great traders) or Algonkian Indians—beads that were used in trade with the English and Dutch. A shilling was worth, on an average, five purple beads. The best wampum articles were the ritual belts made by the Iroquois. They were made as gifts to be given at the time of treaty signings, in funeral ceremonies, and as

Arapaho child in bead-embroidered leather garments. Field Museum of Natural History.

atonements for sins. A hereditary keeper was charged with preserving belts of significance to the Iroquois League.

Wampum belts were woven by women on long parallel strands of leather, string, or vegetable fiber. These strands were kept evenly spaced by means of a leather spacer with holes, which was attached to each end of a bow, upon which the strings were stretched taut. Beads were worked between the strands, the string upon which they were strung acting as a weft. One bead was set between each warp and its neighbor. Belts were 2 to 15 inches wide and 1 to 6 feet in length. An average belt was 4 to 6 inches wide and composed of between one and two thousand beads; a rare belt had seven thousand. The ends of the belt were finished with fringes.

Clusters of foot-long strings of beads were made, but it is not certain what their purpose was, except that they were used in connection with marriage contracts. Abalone, clam, and oyster shells were used for beads. Beads also were made from quartz, magnetite, slate, soapstone, and silver, as well as dried berries and pits. In the north and central plains, Indians carved beads from deer, goat, and sheep horns, and from the bones of turkeys. Bone beads were about an inch long.

The colors of the beads had symbolic meanings. White signified peace, good health, and similar desirable things. Purple meant sorrow. Red was the sign of war (see *Main Types of Sewn Beadwork* by Frederic H. Douglas). Animal teeth, dentalia and cowrie shells, and dried berries and pits were used in their natural colors. Purple shells were used for eastern wampum. The turquoise stones of the Southwest were bright accents. The reds and oranges seen in the Southwest were imported coral. Of course, most shell beads were white. Significantly, white also was the most common color when glass and porcelain beads were substituted for those of natural origin. The only Indians who ever attempted to make glass beads were the Hidatsa, Mandan, and Arikara of North Dakota. Their beads were quite large. All other tribes used glass and porcelain beads imported from Europe when they were available. Porcelain beads came, at first, from Czechoslovakia, Austria, and Venice; glass beads came from Venice and Bavaria. Bohemian glass beads were slightly darker than the Venetian ones, semitransparent, and bluish. Later, beads were imported from Franch and England, and later still, from Japan and Germany.

Beadwork was carried west by fur-trading companies in search of new territories. Eastern Indians, hired as guides and trappers, had taken the floral style to the eastern plains by 1800. In the mid-1800s some Great Lakes and eastern tribes were moved to Okla-

Blackfoot dress beaded in lazy
stitch. Field Museum of Natural
History.

Man's shirt beaded in spot stitch.
The belt is plaited and beaded. Fox.
Field Museum of Natural History.

homa, and thereafter, beadwork was practiced in the Southwest. After the Civil War the railroad was a factor in spreading the craft. By 1870 the Montana Blackfoot were making beadwork, and by 1880 the Tlingit of southeastern Alaska were doing it as well and the craft was already well established among the Indians of the interior.

Beadwork was used to decorate heavy buffalo hides, soft skins of deer and elk, and of course, cloth. Tepees, saddles, saddle covers, shields, and cradleboards were decorated with beadwork. Octopus bags, so called because of the eight appendages dangling from them, were another background for beading. The bag shown in Plate 1 is 42½ inches long and made of trade felt with a plaid lining and a design in polychrome trade beads. It was probably made by Athabaskan Indians, although apparently collected among the Tlingit, who prized bags of this type. Beading was used also for dresses, shirts, leggings, robes, moccasins, pipe bags, scabbards, small bags, and dolls. The Mohegan Indians of Connecticut beaded birchbark. Usually the sections of the article were beaded before assembly. Moccasins are an example of this practice, and often only the vamp was beaded.

Motifs

Indian beadwork, like European beading, was at its peak between 1880 and 1900. Lazy and overlay stitches held the beads in place and were worked close together, which was possible with smaller beads. The Sioux, Cheyenne, and Arapaho used lazy stitch. Overlay was used by the Blackfoot, Sarsi, Plains, Cree, and Flathead. The Crow, Shoshoni, Assiniboin, and Gros Ventre used both stitches.

The Plains Indians usually made beading that was worked solidly within an area. Only in later years did they make the motif-against-background work done by the Great Lakes and Mississippi valley Indians. Presumably teachers in government schools were responsible for the transmission of this technique.

Popular Plains Indian motifs were solid triangles, hourglasses (two triangles joined at the tips), stepped hourglasses, circles, crosses, and oblongs in narrow strips.

In the central plains a great Sioux style emerged, featuring slender, spreading motifs on a solid ground. Isosceles and right triangles, hourglasses, lozenges, pronged forks (made with thin lines), stripes, and bars alternated with oblings were its motifs. These were widely spaced and joined with narrow lines, so that the effect was very much lighter than the designs of many other tribes. The background usually was white. Sioux Indians are said to have

Typical Crow shoulder bag design, a style used also by the Bannock and Shoshoni. The dotted line at the right marks the center of the symmetrical design. Traditionally, beads in pastel shades were sewn in spot stitch to red wool cloth, with white beads for outlines. Completed pouches had ornamented straps extending from the section at left, and fringes along the bottom.

Plains Indian pipe bag ornamented with beads and quillwork. Field Museum of Natural History.

admired Caucasian rugs, which are generally boldly geometrical in design. Cheyenne, Arapaho, and Ute styles of beadwork are similar to those of the Sioux.

The Northern Crow, Shoshoni, and Bannock Indians made great triangles of beading on a background of red cloth. Within the large tall or flat triangles were other triangles or oblongs. Lozenges and hourglasses were made from paired triangles. A vertical banding with bars is typical. White was used only for narrower bars and outlining. The favorite colors were lavender and pale blue. Dark blue, greens, and yellows appeared to a lesser extent. Red was least used. This geometric style later was abandoned in favor of floral patterns.

The Blackfoot style consisted of many squares or rectangles arranged to form larger squares, lozenges, crosses, or slanting bands. In composition the work was dominated by a very large main motif in a single color, banded with squares of contrasting colors. The background was white. Other Indians that used the same type of composition were the Plains, Cree, Sarsi, Flathead, and some of the Assiniboin. The style, which was much like quillwork, was fully developed by the 1880s. Since all sorts of beads were readily available by this time, the areas covered with decoration were enlarged.

The Cheyenne and Arapaho used lazy stitch in limited color combinations to make tall stepped triangles and horizontal stripes, usually in dark colors on white. The Utes used the same basic design but added more motifs, and their color combinations were closer in value.

The Indians of the southern plains acquired horses from the Spanish in the seventeenth century, and by the second quarter of the eighteenth century agricultural tribes along the Mississippi were using them. Once horses were available, hunting tribes became dominant, and the fur trade was established.

Actually, the warbonnet was worn only by the Plains Indians, a confederation of tribes from five different linguistic stocks, all engaged in the fur trade. The fabrication of clothing, tepee covers, and rawhide containers was the work of the women, who were also responsible for the quillwork, beadwork, silk embroidery, and some of the painted, conventional, geometric designs. Articles for the hunt, warfare, and ceremonies were made by men. Skins were prepared in their natural white, were smoked brown, or were dyed black. Fur traders brought cloth, which was used after 1850. Indians preferred coarse fabrics to silk, according to a letter written to the English geographer Richard Hakluyt by Sir Ralph Lane, who led Sir Walter Raleigh's colonizing expedition of 1585 on Roanoke Island.

Design derived from the lower
panel of an Ojibwa beaded cloth
bandoleer bag in the Smithsonian
Institution. The original is 43 by
11½ inches and has a simple beaded
floral pattern in the upper section.
The strap and broad fringes are
worked in simple geometric designs.

60 Chippewa woman doing beadwork.
Field Museum of Natural History.

Design for a strapless bag adapted
from an Ojibwa or Eastern Sioux
original in the Denver Art Museum.
The flower designs were beaded in
spot stitch on black velvet, with a
beaded fringe along the lower edge.

Osage bead loom. Field Museum of Natural History.

61

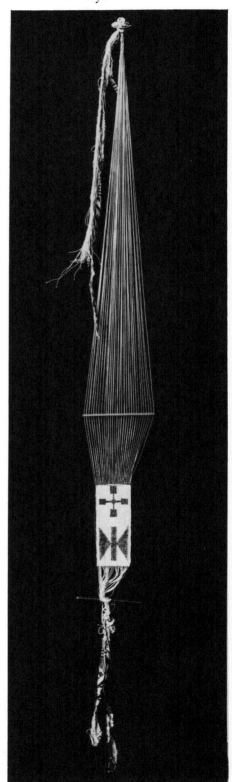

Great Lakes and eastern Indians used beads for borders and for small trims on hide or cloth. Starting perhaps as early as 1700 and continuing until the middle of the next century, they worked white bead patterns in straight or zigzag parallel rows that created chain or lacelike effects. The Indians of New England made patterns in double curves on black, red, or dark-blue cloth. Examples from the late nineteenth century have a crowded, raised effect reminiscent of European metallic embroidery. This type of work was made by the Penobscot and Passamaquoddy Indians of Maine and Canada. The Iroquois and Huron made linear, lacelike patterns with white beads or bands of contrasting colors. The parallel rows forming the design were either straight or zigzag, or the two alternated; they were set closely together so that the tips of the angles touched adjacent rows, producing a meshlike effect.

About mid-nineteenth century multicolored botanical patterns with varying degrees of naturalism appeared, at first worked against white in overlay stitch. Although the design was basically symmetrical, the craftsman usually violated the symmetry at some points. Motifs of this type were made by many tribes, but the Ojibwa displayed especial enthusiasm.

Another name by which the Ojibwa are widely known, Chippewa, is a corruption of the word *ojibway* or *odjibwe*, meaning puckered, which—according to some authorities—refers to the stitching of the particular type of moccasins worn by these Algonkian Indians, who lived in the Upper Michigan and Lake Superior regions. They made some beadwork from an early date in the lacy white patterns already described. Later, they made conventionalized and geometric patterns, weaving them in a frame. Apparently some of these designs were derived from quillwork or bitten patterns.

The Ojibwa made large shoulder bags, garters, headbands, and belts using these woven designs. The bags were woven from split tamarack roots, bark twine, or ravelings from old blankets. In addition to beading, the Ojibwa made birchbark articles decorated with quillwork and colored grasses and a dramatic type of ribbon appliqué.

Most Indian children spent the first year of their lives on a cradleboard. These boards were made of various materials in a variety of shapes by the different tribes. Frequently making them was a matter of family pride and rivalry; each mother wanted the most beautiful carrier for her child. As the tribes migrated or were moved westward by the government, the floral designs they had been making were carried with them and were adopted by the tribes gathered in Oklahoma and those of the southeastern plains.

Octopus bag design adapted from
an Athapaskan example in the
Smithsonian. The original was made
of trade felt with cotton backing,
calico lining, and multicolored
beads.

62

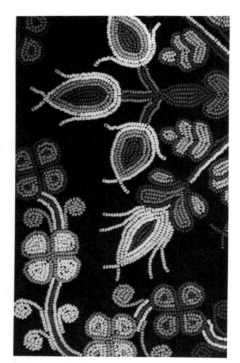

Floral motifs in spot stitch.

Although only a limited amount of beadwork was done by them,
they did completely cover bags and baby carriers with beads, and
these exceptions are thought to date from the period after the
Arapaho and the Southern Cheyenne were moved to Oklahoma.
Foreign patterns infiltrated, but did not dominate, the design of
northern Indians.

Notes on technique

Sinew was used to sew beads to skin, and cotton thread was used to
sew them to cloth. As in making quillwork, a hole was punched in
the skin, and a dampened sinew with a dry, rolled, needlelike
point was put through it to make the stitch. Holes were made with
a steel or bone awl.

Two stitches were used in beadwork, each giving its own effect.
To make lazy stitch, common in the central plains and elsewhere,
a number of beads, perhaps seven, were strung onto the thread or
sinew and sewn into the ground as one stitch. Another group of
beads was then laid alongside it. Eventually an entire area was
filled with short parallel rows of beads. With this arrangement it
was possible to render designs exactly like some of those made with
quills (for which beads, once they were available, were an easily
worked substitute). Often the beads were pushed tightly together
so that each row arched slightly when sewn into place. Usually rows
were made very close together and entirely covered the foundation.

Lazy stitch was not appropriate for the curvilinear designs of
eastern tribes and others; another stitch was needed. Overlay, or
spot, stitch was made by stringing beads on a thread and then
couching this thread onto the design, a stitch between each bead.
Sometimes the close-laid beads gave the appearance of a miniature
mosaic. Undulating lines and detail were possible with this technique. (It should be added that examination of a number of pieces
will show that couching stitches were not always made between
every bead.)

The best achievements in beadwork came from the northern
and central plains. Paintings and written records indicate that little
beadwork was done in this region before 1835–40. The type of bead
used is a clue in dating the item. Earlier beads were about ⅛ inch in
diameter; this was about twice as large as the beads introduced in
1830, which were ¹⁄₁₆ to ³⁄₃₂ inch in diameter. The oldest beads are
irregular. They were faceted as well as round; tubular beads are
of a later date. Translucent beads came into use about 1875; before
that only opaque beads were used. By 1885 metal beads or
glass beads coated with silver or silver gilt were available.

Octopus bag in spot stitch, adapted from an Athapaskan example. Made by V. C. Bath.

White and medium-blue beads were the favorite colors, with black in third place. (These were the cheapest and most profitable to the trader, it should be added. Even today ceramic and glass workers pay more for reds and yellows.) Buff, red shades, dark blues, and a translucent red over white also were used. Early beads were called pony beads, because they were brought to the Indians by pack ponies. The journal of the Lewis and Clark Expedition mentions this type of bead.

In the early period lazy stitch was used, worked loosely, and only sinew was used for sewing. Designs were simple isosceles triangles pendant from a bar or stripe, zigzagged bars, alternating bars and oblongs, or concentric oblongs. The patterns were bold and simple. Large areas of beading were not used; a band 6 inches wide is unusual. The work generally appeared on men's shirts or women's yokes.

Beadwork is a much less taxing craft than quillwork. Experiments in both lazy stitch and spot stitch are shown here. Lazy stitch, especially when worked in borders and around curves, clearly shows a relationship to quillwork design. In practice, it also is apparent that there is a relationship between lazy stitch and loom-woven beaded ornaments. In each the pattern is counted out in beads and builds as successive rows are applied. For the sample the motif selected was based on right triangle/isosceles triangle designs on a Sioux vest in the Denver Art Museum. Guidelines were marked with tracing wheel and paper on a base of man-made leather. Perpendicular lines at intervals would help to keep stitches properly upright. Drawing the design on the ground is futile. It is best to start in the center and work outward, counting out beads in appropriate colors to make the design. In the example, stitches were crowded with an extra bead to make them arch slightly, as they do in Indian beadwork.

Spot, or overlay, stitch was used to make the designs on an octopus bag based on an Athabaskan example in the Smithsonian Institution. Beads were strung on one thread, and a second thread was used to couch them into place on their black ground. The beads were sewn first along the contours of the motifs. All the beading was done in this way, except along the edges of the bag, where beads were worked into buttonhole stitches.

Beads generally available today are much larger than those used by the Indians and not so carefully graded. To see just what the difference actually is, we purchased beads from a store that is part of a national chain. Only one size was available. Motifs were worked in almost the same way as on the original Smithsonian

Working lazy stitch.

Lazy stitch.

Spot or overlay stitch.

example, except that in most cases there was one less row of beads. The original bag is 22 inches long; the adaptation measures 31 inches in length.

Many Indian garments were decorated with narrow bands of loom-woven beads. Bead weaving is an easy craft that can be done in several ways. A simple loom can be built, but it also is possible to use a piece of stiff cardboard of appropriate length, taped at the ends so that threads will not snag on it. The finished beaded band can be twice as long as the cardboard, if made in a continuous ring, or if cut, any shorter length. If twelve beads are to be woven across the width of the band, thirteen warps will be needed, so sturdy thread is wrapped around the cardboard thirteen times and tied. Masking tape at the bottom will keep the threads from slipping. A ruler makes a good tool to lift the warps. Twelve beads, arranged in pattern, are threaded and the needle slipped *under* the warps, the ruler providing a passage. One bead is positioned between each warp and its neighbor. Next, the needle is slipped through each bead and *on top* of each warp, returning it to the starting point. The following row is made in the same way. A usual finish, if the band is to be used for a belt or necklace, is to thread beads onto each warp, making a beaded fringe.

Embroidery

The Pueblo woman's main article of clothing was a rectangle of hand-woven cloth, a manta, which was worn either as a shawl or wrapped into a dress. Before the coming of the Spaniards it was white cotton. After the Spaniards had introduced sheep, it was black wool.

An outstanding type of embroidery was made by the Pueblo Indians of New Mexico and Arizona, in a version of split stitch in two-ply woolen yarn. As the needle was brought to the surface for each stitch, it split the plies of the previous stitch. Designs are said to be "negative," or "reserved," when the background is solidly filled with stitches and the motifs are formed by the ground cloth showing through the stitched areas. The stitches were sewn in horizontal rows, giving the work a brocaded look. The nature and arrangement of the designs suggests pre-Columbian textiles. In 1582–83 Antonio de Espejo, a Mexican merchant, is said to have obtained four thousand blankets in the Moqui (Hopi) towns. His journal mentions garments with colored threads and painted decorations. The use of the word *bordado* seems to indicate that early cotton garments were embroidered.

Oraibi embroidered ceremonial
robe. Field Museum of Natural
History.

68 Acoma embroidered shawl. Field
Museum of Natural History.

The Pueblo Indians, were, of course, preeminent weavers, and the same types of patterns that were made in embroidery also can be found in laid-in weaving and brocading. The earliest existing work is wool on wool or wool on cotton in simple stripe designs. More complex patterns seem to be later developments.

It is believed that the Indians found large masses of dark color unattractive and therefore lightened such areas with designs in reserve.

Pueblo men decorated mantas using hand-spun three-ply (and later, four-ply) yarn on hand-woven cloth. The technique reaches its peak on the black woolen garments of the Acoma and Laguna Indians.

The embroidery often was made with the ravelings of trade cloth. The Indians were fond of a material called baize by the English and bayeta by the Spanish. They liked the red lake color with which it sometimes was dyed. Commercial yarns also were used, and when they were, they give a clue to the age of the piece. The oldest of the needleworks have embroidery in black with greenish yellow and, sometimes, indigo. A rare piece has a cochineal red. Definite greens and browns are commercial dye.

This type of embroidery continued longest among the Hopi. Pueblo wool weaving began early in the seventeenth century, after sheep had been introduced. Men were the weavers. Often a cloth intended for embroidery was woven with tabby (plain) weave at the ends, where embroidery was to be made, and twill weave over the rest of the area. Bands of embroidery in negative, or reserved, designs—usually a motif repeated along the band—were broken at intervals with vertical stripes or pairs of stripes in a contrasting color.

Floral designs also were used. These are thought to be of Mexican origin. The flowers were rendered in flat stitch. The Acoma and Laguna Indians preferred complex designs in red, blue, and green, with red dominating. The Zuñi used simple floral patterns, favoring blue embroidery on a black ground. Various European stitches found their way into this work.

Notes on technique

Embroidered Indian designs of the type made in the Southwest should be worked on tabby-woven cloth, so that the verticals, horizontals, and diagonals reserved as the pattern can be made with precision. These are thread-counted embroideries. Woolen thread with two distinct plies or two threads twisted together are embroidered as in making split stitch, each stitch splitting the plies of the last.

Appliqué

Appliqué techniques were used by Indians in many places, but the art developed most fully in the Great Lakes area. The Menominee Indians, known to the white men since 1634, made appliqués of an inlaid and counterchanged type. This work is thought to have Spanish origins. There are similarities both in technique and in color between the Menominee and Penobscot appliqués, the patchworks of the Seminole, and the reversed, or inlaid, appliqués of the *molas* of the Cuna Indians of Panama's San Blas Islands. Menominee appliqués were designed as wide strips of reciprocating colors. The article may have two or more pairs of stripes in the decorative unit. The color that is the background in one stripe of the pair is the color of the motif (or top layer) on the other stripe. The Penobscot used rows of beads to define the edges of their appliqués.

The palette used by the northern Indians was similar to that used by the Seminole and the Cuna: red, black, cerise, turquoise, yellow, blue, and white. The Potawatomi, who, like the Menominee, were in the Wisconsin area, were equally exuberant in their choices of colors: purple, blue, red, green, cerise, white, and the like. The paired colors in the silk-ribbon appliqués of the Menominee and others were used in bands that ran vertically up the front of the skirt as well as along the edges of skirts and shawls. The Cuna used the same colors, favoring red, in the same type of striking juxtapositions, if for different types of designs. The allover, horizontally striped, geometric patchworks of the Seminole stressed red, pink, and black. Sac and Fox Indians made reciprocal appliqués. Another appliqué technique was used by the San Cordos Apache; they laid leather cutouts over red cloth.

Silk appliqué was being made by the Woodland Indians in the middle of the eighteenth century. Most of it was done by Indian women for their own clothing, but some leggings for men were decorated with it, and it was used for cradleboard wrappings and moccasin ornamentation. For the earliest work silk ribbons were used. Later, ordinary fabric was cut into strips. Aside from the Menominee and Prairie Potawatomi, other Indians practiced the art: the Miami, Kickapoo, Sac and Fox, Winnebago, and Forest Potawatomi.

Birchbark appliqué was made by the Indians of the northeastern United States and Canada. The material was collected and prepared as in other birchbark crafts. In early work dyed spruce roots were used for the sewing, for the bindings, and for embroidering outlines. In Maine and New Brunswick the double-curve style

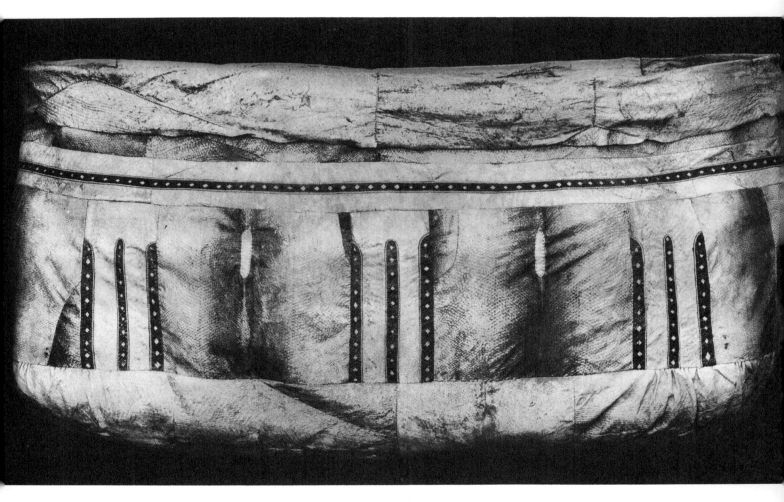

with floral designs and animals was rendered in bark on bark appliqué. In modern work the sewing is done with raffia.

Eskimo bag. Fishskin patchwork and appliqué. Field Museum of Natural History.

Notes on technique
Ribbon appliqués are difficult to make with the stiff ribbons generally available today. Try to find soft silk ribbons or cut strips of cloth. For a patterned band two lengths each of two contrasting colors are needed. The foundation is made by appliquéing two of the lengths, one of each color, adjacent to one another. Over each color the contrasting length is basted and overcast along the outer edge. In old work most of the designs were made by cutting slits in the abutting edges at right angles or obliquely, and then folding under the cut edges in various ways and overcasting.

Aleut bag made of walrus and seal intestines and dyed skin and trimmed with colored yarn and eagle down. Sheldon Jackson Museum.

Patchworks

Patchworks were made by the eastern Aleuts, who fashioned water-proof garments of seal intestines, dried and cut into strips, then carefully sewn together and decorated with painted designs. In other areas intestines of bear or deer were used. Smaller items, such as pouches and mittens, were made of fishskins. In the Sheldon Jackson Museum in Sitka, there are a hood and a parka made of salmon skin.

Parkalike garments called *kamleikas* were made by western Eskimos in northern Alaska (from the Bering Strait and Point Barrow to the Yukon). Decoration sometimes beading, was concentrated at the seams. Sometimes the skins were dyed; natural skins are almost white with an interesting translucent texture. One garment has red-dyed skins combined with natural skins, the seams featherstitched in navy thread. Sometimes two layers of skin were used, the top layer cut to show the layer below. Often contrasting stitching was used. Trimmings were concentrated at the hems or emanated from the seams. The narrow intestines generally were joined to make an effect of horizontal striping. Fur, shells, teeth, feathers, and beads were the usual ornaments. A more striking decoration was the feathered crest of the crested auklet.

Although color was used sparingly, fishskin and intestine pieced work is dramatic and sophisticated. The garments have a crinkly, shirred effect, but the clothing was expertly tailored and the skins well arranged, with an eye for beauty as well as utility.

Eskimo and Aleut also made decorative parkas from cormorants, puffins, and other sea birds and animals, using leather, ermine, sea otter, eagle down, cloth, and beads for trimmings.

Alaskan women used bone needles. Their needle cases and awls were delicately carved and their thimble was a circle of leather with an off-center slit in it. The finger was put through the slit, and the broad side of the circle positioned to protect the finger. They eschewed European thimbles for sewing and kept new metal thimbles offered to them to use as ornaments for their needlework. For thread, they used grasses, roots, or the sinews of reindeer legs.

The Haidas of British Columbia made appliqué blankets and garments in simple patterns with strong, contrasting colors. The unusual features of these articles were their borders and figures made of rows of dentalium shells and commercial shell buttons.

At the opposite end of the Continent were the Seminole, whose patchworks were made in bands. Tiny triangles, squares, and lozenges in bright colors were arranged in repeated sequences. Stitching on old work is very fine. The general effect of these patchworks can be obtained by machine stitching together strips of cotton cloth of various colors and widths and joining them along the long sides. Cut these into small segments and arrange them with other segments, similarly made, to create a repeated design. Bands of plain colored cotton cloth should separate the patterned bands.

Seminole Indians wearing traditional patchworks. Field Museum of Natural History.

Salmon-skin parka. Eskimo, Yukon territory. Sheldon Jackson Museum. Photograph by Alice Postell.

II Surface Embroidery in Woolen Thread

Surface Embroidery
in Woolen Thread

"Adam and Eve" worked by Mary
Sarah Titcomb. 1760. Wadsworth
Atheneum, J. J. Goodwin Fund.

Crewel (also spelled crewell, crewels, cruel, cruell, croull, croole, and crool) is slackly plied worsted thread. The term probably comes from the Anglo-Saxon *cleowen*, meaning ball of thread. Crewels can be used for many kinds of embroidery, including various types of thread-counted needlework on soft or stiff canvas or tabby-woven linen, as well as for surface stitching. Today "crewel embroidery" usually refers to surface stitching with woolen threads, but using the term in this way can lead to confusion, because historically, crewel embroidery is any needlework made with the particular type of worsted thread called crewel. Surface embroidery is an awkward and little-used phrase, but it clearly defines a broad category of needlework in which the manner of inserting stitches into the ground cloth has no particular relation to its weave, but follows a drawing on the surface of the cloth. Generally such embroidery incorporates a variety of stitches, frequently chosen for the degree of relief they produce. In surface needlework all stitches create a raised texture, but the effect varies, and part of the charm of the embroidery lies in the manner in which relief is managed.

Surface embroidery is an ancient technique. Bronze Age garments of embroidered wool are preserved in Scandinavian countries, and embroidered woolen garments were made in Greece four centuries before Christ. Before the mid-fourteenth century and the years of plague, English ecclesiastical emboidery in silk (and to some extent in metal), called *opus anglicanum,* was one of the reigning Western arts. When the break with the Roman Catholic church came (1534–40), much needlework was transferred to domestic use, influencing Tudor wives, who from the time of Elizabeth I made, or supervised the making of, great amounts of clothing and articles for the house: wall hangings, cushions, bed furniture (bed hangings), bedcovers, and table and floor carpets.

Several factors contributed to the rise of domestic embroidery in England. The distribution of the holdings of the monasteries after their dissolution put ordinary embroiderers into intimate touch with the best of ecclesiastical work. The success of merchant fleets had

Multiflowered columnar pattern typical of eighteenth-century American embroidery.

Picture worked in crewels. New England, 1725–1800. Henry Francis du Pont Winterthur Museum.

added to the ranks of the recently affluent. Even the availability of steel needles may have been a factor. It is believed that Islamic needleworkers brought steel needles into Europe during the fourteenth century. Until the middle of the sixteenth century English embroiderers used bone needles or imported steel needles. Steel needles from Spain or Germany became available in England during Mary Tudor's reign (1553–58). English manufacture followed, and by mid-seventeenth century there was an English needlemakers' guild.

In the seventeenth century an incredible amount of professional, semiprofessional, and domestic needlework was completed in England. The earliest American pieces are the direct descendants of this needlework—some pieces are indistinguishable from it—in a style called Jacobean, although it came later than Jacobean design in other objects. Of course, some of the embroidery used in the colonies was made in England, and many of the pieces worked in America were designs drawn in England on cloth of English manufacture. The importance of the influence of English—and European —design upon the embroidery of America can hardly be overstressed. Before noting how New World designs developed, it might be well to have a look at English and European motifs.

English and European Designs in the New World
Embroidery made during the reign of Elizabeth I (1558–1603) featured the rose, pineapple, pomegranate, strawberry, potato flower (common in Portuguese work also), coiling stems, and designs within diapered compartments. One design book popular in England in the late sixteenth century contained patterns for 124 birds, 16 animals, and 52 fishes. Flowers were stylized, but animals, birds, and insects were rendered naturalistically. Pattern books gave no guidance in the matter of shading or of what stitches should be used; these decisions were left to the embroiderer. The favorite colors of the time for silk embroidery were shades of blue, green, pale yellow, pink, crimson, and black, white for woolen embroidery the choices were more apt to be dark blues, greens, reds, oranges, yellows, and browns.

Early Jacobean or Stuart embroidery was much the same, with many flowers, birds, and plants. Carnations, roses, and potato flowers were popular motifs. During the Restoration the oak, associated with Charles I, appeared. Embroidery colors became brilliant, with jasmine, cherry, harebell, and honeysuckle prominent among the flowers. Designs came from woven fabrics, manuscript illumination, pattern books like the popular *A Schole-house for the Needle* by

80

Patterns derived from the Mary
Fifield bed hangings. Reciprocal
curves, spiny contour, and patterned
in-filling of leaves are typical of
seventeenth-century English
embroidery. (See page 88.)

Richard Shorleyker (1624), Thomas Trevelyon's *Commonplace Book* (1608) and *Chronicle* (1616), Bibles, botanical and zoological books, engravings, and wall and lining papers. Engravings by Peter Stent, John Overton, and others also provided subjects.

The use of biological themes reflected the growing interest in the natural world in the seventeenth and eighteenth centuries. Two of the best-known books with illustrations of animals were Edward Topsell's *Historie of Four-Footed Beastes and Serpents* (1606) and Thomas Moffett's (or Moufet's) *Insectorum* (1634). Konrad von Gesner's books on plants and animals also were widely distributed. Herbals were of great importance.

In the seventeenth century English hand-blocked papers had rather small floral motifs. These changed after the English began importing large rolls of hand-painted paper from China. The usual Chinese design showed a large flowering, many-branched tree. Also increasingly influential were palampores, large painted and printed cloths imported from India, which usually showed a similar motif. Palampores were used in England, America, and elsewhere as bedcovers and sometimes as curtains, and from them British and American embroiderers derived many of their designs.

The Jacobean style continued through the William and Mary period, but designs of the Queen Anne period (1702–14) were smaller and more widely spaced. In the colonies spacing was broader and drawing more free. The English rose, thistle, and carnation were mingled with elements translated from designs on porcelain and textiles that had been brought to the West by the East India Company. The carnation, besides being a popular English flower, was used widely in Persian design, which was influencing England in this period. Fantastic and even grotesque patterns that had evolved during the previous period were dropped. In America some of the blue and white designs that developed are thought to have been inspired by Canton ware brought to New England via the China trade.

The graceful naturalism of the Queen Anne period continued until the Hanoverian period (which began in 1714), when German patterns came into favor.

Symbolism played a part in the choice of embroidery designs. In England, the Scottish thistle, the prince's feather, and the Irish trefoil were staple motifs. The rose became a favorite motif during Elizabethan times: the white rose, or musk rose, of the Yorks, the red rose of the Lancasters, and the Tudor rose. There were emblems and badges of rank. In the sixteenth century a number of emblem books were published, containing family badges, heraldic symbols,

Simple leaf from Fifield bed hangings.

and devices with phrases dedicated to moral uplift. Scrolls and figures were to be found on legal documents drawn up by the Scriveners' Company. In the process of rearranging and simplifying these designs for embroidery, patternmakers often obscured the source. Shops sold their designs, drawn on paper or inked onto cloth, ready for work.

Apparently there was no lack of class consciousness in the New World, but in time the symbols of independence prevailed— on furniture, pottery, glass, and textiles. The motifs included the tea leaf, the American rose, the rising sun, the pine tree, the arms of the union and of various states, the Stars and Stripes, the bald eagle, the figures of Columbia and Liberty, portraits of national heroes, and illustrations of important national events. The presence of these symbols can help in dating a piece. However, not many of the symbols are to be found in surface embroidery in wool, a technique that declined with the Revolution. They are more often found in silk embroidery, which came later.

Cotton cloth came into use as a ground fabric, replacing earlier combinations of linen and cotton or all linen. Chain stitch, popular on Oriental embroidery, replaced the earlier self-couched and flat-stitched techniques to some extent. The favorite motif of the eighteenth cenutry was the basket of flowers; by mid-century its popularity amounted to a craze.

Center motif from the Adams christening blanket. (See page 90.)

Illustration from John Gerard's *The Herball.*

Harebells.

Woodbine.

Musk rose.

Illustrations from *La Clef des Champs*.

Illustrations from *La Clef des Champs*.

Gardens and herbals were an important source of embroidery design. Damask roses, rose campions, carnations (geliflowers or gillyflowers), irises or flowers de-luce, peonies, pansies (pawnsees or *pensées*), daffodils, violets, hyacinths, bluebells (harebells), honeysuckle (called woodbine), cornflowers (bluebottles), daisies, and borage were all subjects for embroidery.

Among the herbals available as pattern sources were John Gerard's *The Herball, or Generall Historie of Plantes*, printed in London in 1597, Otto Brunfels's *Herbarum Vivae Eicones*, published in Strasbourg in 1530, the *Rariorum Plantarum Historia* (1601) of Charles de l'Ecluse, the copperplate engravings of Crispijn van de Passe in *Hortus Floridus* (1614–16), and the woodcuts in Jacques le Moyne's (or Lemoine's) *La Clef des Champs pour trouver plusieurs animaux, etc.*, published in London in 1586. Le Moyne's *La Clef des Champs* and sets of watercolors by him were used widely by designers in many crafts besides embroidery.

Oriental Motifs

The mercantile activities of European traders had a vital effect on English and American embroidery design. The Portuguese established themselves at Calicut (today Kozhikode) in 1510 and in Goa in 1515; by 1517 they were trading with China and in 1550 had possessions in Persia, Ceylon, Indochina, and the Malay Archipelago.

By the late sixteenth century Chinese materials, including textiles, began to reach the West, and by the seventeenth century they began to have an important impact. By the eighteenth century Europe and England were well acquainted with Chinese silks, porcelains, lacquers, prints, painted papers, painted glass, and enamels. From about 1700 on imported cloth, both silk and Indian cotton, was worn by fashionable women, including royalty. By the second half of the century Oriental articles were the height of fashion, and European and English designers had begun to imitate their effects.

The English East India Company was granted charters by Elizabeth I in 1600 and by Cromwell in 1657. Its first contacts were with India. In 1715 the company opened a manufactory in Canton, which, after 1757, was the only Chinese port open to foreign traders. Among the workshops, or hongs, were the American Factory and the New England Factory. Sometimes the craftsmen were overseen by European foremen, and sometimes European or English designs were used. As a result, styles became intermingled.

The East India Company was charged to bring back textiles of various weaves, plain, flowered, and embroidered. Some of the orders were private commissions for bedcovers and hangings and garments.

The East India Company imported not only Chinese silks, but also fine polychrome silk embroidery from India. The chain stitch used on this work soon attracted the interest of eighteenth-century embroiderers. It has been possible in a few cases to match an embroidery with a painted and printed cloth of the same design.

Western delight in the silk emboidery of the Chinese probably is one of the reasons for the decline of woolen embroidery in the West as the century progressed. The Chinese used satin stitch, long and short stitch, and Peking stitch, which became the French knot when worked abroad. This stitch is appropriately called texture stitch or accent stitch at times.

By 1700 an act had been passed forbidding the use of Indian, Persian, or Chinese silks in England, in an effort to protect the domestic silk-weaving industry, which was becoming important.

Bluebottles. Illustration from *La Clef des Champs*.

Detail of the bed curtain shown on page 85.

Vertical border showing the use of self-couching (Roumanian stitch). The design was adapted from a bed curtain in the collection of the Art Institute of Chicago. Made by the author.

Bed curtain and valance. Early eighteenth century. A detail of the valance is shown in color in Plate 5. Art Institute of Chicago, gift of Mrs. Albert H. Barber.

In Lyons, the great French textile center, importation of silks had been forbidden even earlier.

The flowering tree motif, which prevailed over a long period, may be of either Eastern or Western origin. The Indian chintz painter sometimes worked from patterns (called musters) sent from the West, sometimes from a Japanese or Chinese prototype. He used delicate resists in indigo, madder, and other colors, sometimes achieving a number of colors in one dyeing by using more than one mordant. If his design was of Chinese origin, the hillocks at the base of the tree were apt to be sharply angled and rocky. The branches of the tree were not covered with flowers. The Chinese permitted themselves blossoms only at the tips of the branches. The shading used by the Chinese painter was interpreted by the chintz maker in a dry-brush effect. He sometimes used the lilies and chrysanthemums favored by the Chinese painter, but if he decorated the branches of his tree with many flowers of different types, he was working with a foreign idea.

Sometimes designs were sent from India to China to be copied by Chinese embroiderers, in whose hands the color of the design would become less wide-ranging and more subdued. Branches would be shorn of most of their leaves and flowers.

Between 1615 and 1619 gifts of English embroidery customarily were sent as gifts to prominent Indians. In this way English embroidery may have influenced Indian needlework. More significant, perhaps, were the patterns sent from the West to be copied by the chintz painters. It has been possible to link some of the finished fabrics with their prototypes. The *Twelve Months of Famous Flowers*, engravings by H. Fletcher made from paintings by Peter Cosleels, a Flemish artist working in England, and published by Robert Furber in 1730, are an example. These engravings originally were published as a Kensington nurseryman's catalogue, one of the first of such books. Furber did not overlook possible indirect uses of the engravings and suggested that they might be helpful to painters, carvers, japanners, and even to "the Ladies." A set can be seen at Colonial Williamsburg, and they have been reproduced widely. This writer recently saw a set at a suburban Sears, Roebuck store.

K. B. Brett, retired curator of textiles at the Royal Ontario Museum, linked the Furber designs to a palampore at that museum. Made between 1730 and 1740, this cover is a combination of painting and resist dyeing in a color scheme of blues, reds, violets, yellows, and blacks, with some yellow painted over blue to produce green. A number of the Fletcher bouquets representing the months

86 Detail of vertical border. The leaf at the upper left is done in long and short stitch.

Border details adapted from the bed curtain shown on page 85.

87

of the year have been copied in the palampore. Except for a slight change in overall shape, and the substitution of bowknots for the vases of the original, the designs are the same. The Indian painter interpreted the detailed lines of the black and white engravings in the flat shapes and colors of his medium in a translation very much like that which an embroiderer would make—simple and with clearly defined areas of color.

It may be that by this circuitous route English and American needleworkers arrived at their patterns. The painting by a Flemish artist, meticulously recording the details of the native flowers of his homeland, as well as exotic imports like the tulip, was redrawn in black and white by an English engraver, whose designs reached an Indian artist, who, working in color, reinterpreted the patterns to make palampores, in the process abstracting them in accordance with his native instinct for two-dimensional representation, as well as the limitations of his technique.

"Bed Furniture" and Other Furnishings

In England until the late fifteenth century beds were set up in the main halls of the great houses. At night they were surrounded by curtains that were drawn up to the ceiling during the day. After separate rooms for sleeping became the fashion, wealthy homes were equipped with sturdy bedframes hung with curtains of the best fabrics a family could afford, for the bedroom was a place to receive guests. Such bed furniture offered a worthy field for the embroiderer's art.

Woolen bed curtains were common, although in the late seventeenth century in England those who could afford it hung their beds with silks of various weaves and with velvet, as well as wool. Sometimes valances were elaborately fringed.

Linen and cotton bed curtains heavily embroidered with crewels probably came into use about the middle of the seventeenth century. Designs were of several types, but the Great Tree, or Tree of Life, was probably the most popular. Sometimes it lost its tree form and appeared only as intertwining, dominantly vertical branches. In either case the foliage and flowers ranged along the branches suggest those of Portuguese painted pintados or Indian palampores. The fanciful trees sprang from decorative hillock borders, where animals cavorted amid the flowers. The elements of the design combine Indian and English motifs with curling leaves of the type seen on Flemish tapestry. Some of the bed curtains were based entirely on these large-leaved blue and green verdure tap-

Leaf pattern derived from Mary Fifield bed hangings.

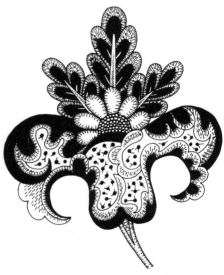

Value arrangement, stitch direction, and patterned filling of the design.

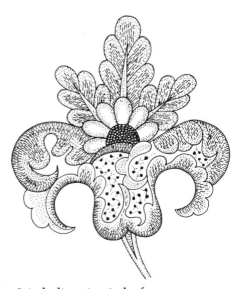

Stitch direction in leaf.

88

Cover made from bed hangings embroidered by Mary Thurston Fifield and Mary Fifield Adams. Boston, ca. 1700–15. Museum of Fine Arts, Boston, gift of Mrs. Joseph Avery Manning.

estries. A vining tendril or coiling stem, expanded in scale, but still enclosing flowers or other motifs, was a less usual design.

In mid-eighteenth-century America the master bed still was in the parlor in many homes. Folding beds, called half tester or half-headed, were also used. These could be folded against the wall with curtains hung from a ceiling frame drawn around them. Houses were small and furniture scarce. Window curtains and floor carpets were seldom seen, but Turkey or canvas work cushions and table covers were common.

Cloth was 18 to 28 inches wide depending on the width of the loom. Two five-breadth curtains were used to surround the foot and lower end of the bed. The curtains at the sides near the head were made of two and one-half or three widths. The Olde Gaol Museum, York, Maine, has a complete set of bed furnishings made by Mary Bulman—bed hangings, cover, headpiece, and valances.

Valances or pelmets were hung straight or stretched, giving an opportunity for illustrative or narrative compositions that would not have been appropriate for the bed curtains. Valances were not always made of embroidery. The Henry Francis du Pont Winterthur Museum has a set made of paper decorated with ink and wash patterns of the same type as those that were worked in embroidery. (It was once thought that the set might have been patterns for needlework, but this idea has been discarded, because all the parts have identical motifs. Moreover, advertisements of the period indicate that paper valances were in use—one type was covered with printed paper.)

Although curtains for windows apparently were not made to match the bed furniture, sometimes sets of chair seats were. The Bradstreet bed curtains and chair seats, for example, seem to have been meant to go together, although they are dissimilar in style and skill of workmanship; the differences suggest that the curtains were made by the mother and the seats by the daughter.

Exactly what the elements of bed "furniture" consisted of is open to question. Obviously, valances and curtains lasted longer than coverlets, so in various cases it is not possible to be sure whether there originally was a matching coverlet or not, unless there is some documentation. Also, by the end of the colonial period styles had changed, and often a full set of bed curtains was not used, only valances and side curtains at the head end. Typically, the ground fabric for bed curtains was fustian, a twill-woven cloth with linen warp and cotton weft. Occasionally, an example existing today will show a bit of nap. If these curtains were embroidered with the same stitches that were used in England, there would be

Christening blanket made by Mary Fifield Adams, ca. 1700–15. Museum of Fine Arts, Boston, gift of Miss Mary Avery White.

Border design from the Adams christening blanket. The left end joins the center-border motif; the right joins the corner. The design reverses to make the left half of the border.

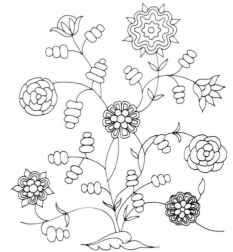

Motif that appears at the center of the border on each of the four sides of the blanket.

no way to distinguish them from those made in the Old World. Such is the case with a set of bed hangings that were made by Mary Thurston Fifield and her daughter, Mary Fifield Adams, ca. 1700–15.

The Fifield bed curtains, later cut to be used as covers, are completely documented to the present. The fustian with the design drawn on it and the worsted with which to work it were brought from England by Captain Richard Fifield of Boston. The mother and daughter worked the pieces in typical heavy English stitching. The designs were Jacobean, but with Oriental elements. The undulating hillock looks quite Chinese. The curling leaves are a staple device of the period. That the curtains belong to the eighteenth rather than the seventeenth century is suggested by the comparatively small scale of the motifs. The Jacobean style continued in fashion until the mid-eighteenth century.

Quite as representative of the eighteenth century as the Fifield bed hangings are other designs, smaller in scale, worked in lighter-weight yarn and, because of the popularity of imported tambours and chain stitch embroideries, done in chain stitch. In these works small sprays were scattered over the area, and dissimilar motifs were repeated in regular sequence, as a rule. Sometimes a wide, related border was added.

It is interesting to note that a christening blanket made by Mary Adams and dated 1700–15 is the same period as the bed hangings but is of completely different character. The motifs are more Persian in feeling, and the layout is consistent with those of Persian covers. According to Anne Pollard Rowe in "Crewel Embroidered Bed Hangings in Old and New England" (Museum of Fine Arts, Boston, *Bulletin*), Mary made the christening blanket as a child, working the designs on the fustian primarily in chain stitch. Probably Mary worked the border, but because her arms were too short to reach the motifs in the center of the framed needlework, her mother embroidered that part. Tradition has it that this was the blanket used for the christening of Samuel Adams, Mary's son, who was born in 1722.

Most colonial American embroidery in crewels was worked with a more limited variety of stitches than are found in English work. Two stitches are predominant. One is the familiar self-couched Roumanian or economy stitch, which also is referred to at times as Oriental stitch, American stitch, and in other countries, with slight variations, by other names. The purpose of the stitch is to cover an area completely with yarn; basically, long stitches are laid across the area, then tied to the ground with couching stitches

Motif that appears in the two lower corners of the blanket, just above the border.

Bed furnishings made by Mary Bulman. York, Maine, ca. 1745. Old Gaol Museum, York.

Symmetrical horizontal design of a
type common in bed furnishings.

Value arrangement for the flowers
of the corner motif of the Adams
christening blanket.

made with the same thread. A great deal of fuss is made about
the length and direction of the stitches used for the couching. A
slight variation is sufficient to call the work by a new name. In
colonial work the stitch was quite long, very slanted, and usually
fairly loose, so that, with the plies of the yarn confusing the eye, it is
easy to mistake the embroidery for flat stitch.

Flat stitch, in colonial crewelwork, is rather like satin stitch,
except that the yarn is not carried across the back in making successive stitches. Instead, the needle is brought up very near to the place
where the last stitch ended and another laid alongside it. Neither
the self-couched technique nor the flat stitching leaves much thread
on the back of the work, which is commonly thought to be the reason why the stitches were so popular. Certainly this is a point to be
considered seriously if a woman must spin and dye her own yarn.
For wealthy women in Boston it must have been a consideration of
less importance. More to the point, perhaps, is the fact that this
stitching, couched or flat, was good looking and worked up rapidly.

However, design remained closest to that of England in the
port cities along the coast, where contact was most direct, and bed
curtains with designs drawn on them ready for work could readily
be ordered from England.

94

Tree motifs illustrate the method
embroiderers used to show the
trunk growing from the soil.

Motifs from the mid-section of the
Adams christening blanket.

There is little evidence that bed curtains made in America were copied from pattern books, nor do many English examples seem to derive from such sources. One set of bed curtains of undetermined origin is an exception. Its linear motifs, small and spotted as if transferred one by one onto the cloth, retain a woodcut feeling. The running dog, the leaping stag, the bird, and the squirrel, repeated over and over across the panels in red crewels, are familiar motifs, although usually they appear in full color rather than in the simple linear expression of these curtains.

The idea that women may have made their own designs is not to be discounted, although most embroidery of the scale of the bed curtains does not seem to have originated in this way. Women seem to have taken motifs from other sources and arranged them, often in a rather ordinary composition, across the expanse of the cloth. The Bulman bed furniture is an exception. Made about 1745, the pieces, worked in crewels on linen, are all quite original in conception, combining heavy flat-stitched Jacobean motifs with the open, airy spacing typical of American work. The central rectangle of the coverlet is bordered with a heavy, undulating stem; in each of its curves is a large boldly colored flower or leaf. The color scheme is dominated by reds, blues (some very deep), and green. Within the surrounding stem are six simple but large floral sprays. The sides of

Embroidered panels, part of a set of
cotton bed hangings worked in red
crewels in outline, blanket, and
seed stitches. Probably English,
late seventeenth century.
Metropolitan Museum of Art,
Rogers Fund, 1940.

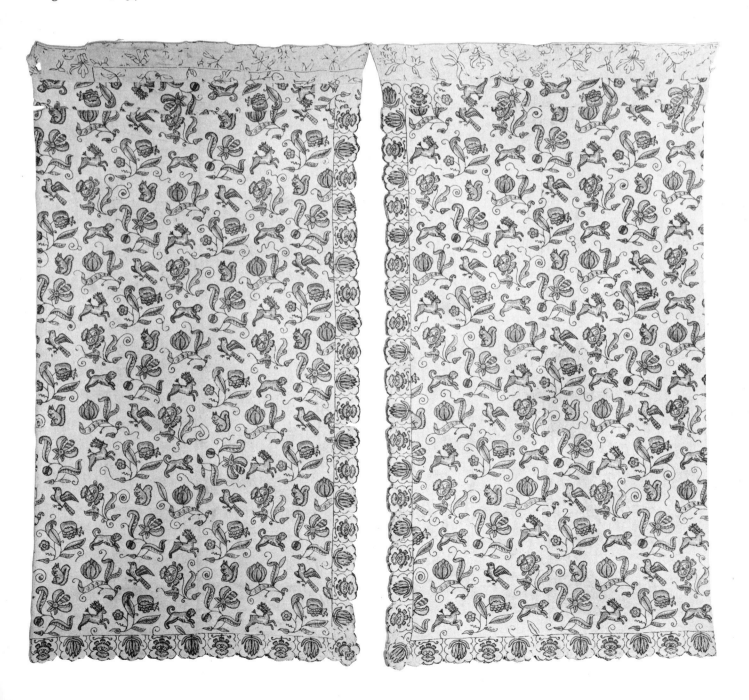

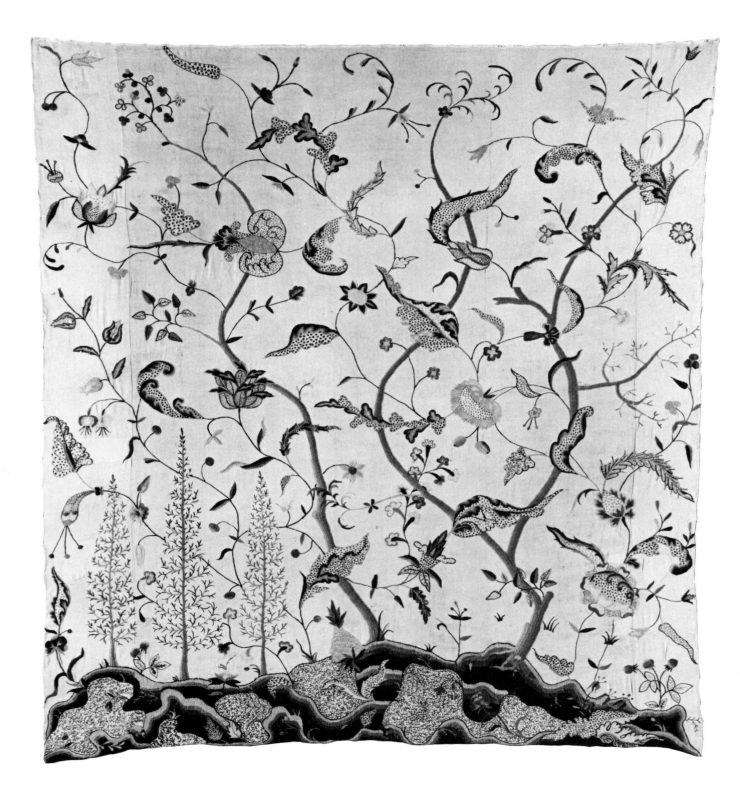

Wide bed curtain, possibly from the Lowell family. Wool on cotton and linen. New England, 1725–50. Museum of Fine Arts, Boston, gift of Ellen W. Coolidge.

the coverlet, shaped to fit the bedstead, are decorated with borders of wavy stems and flowers also, but smaller in scale.

The most unusual feature of the set, the only complete set to have survived, is the poem embroidered on the valances. It is "Meditation in a Grove," by the Reverend Isaac Watts, from *Horae, Lyricae,* written in 1706; it begins:

Sweet Muse, descend and bless the Shade,
And bless the Evening Grove;
Business, and Noise, and Day are fled,
And every Care, but Love.

The verses take on special significance, as do the boldness and gaiety of the embroidery, when we consider the circumstances under which this needlework was made. According to tradition, Mary Bulman began this monumental task in order to keep herself occupied. Her husband, a surgeon serving under Sir William Pepperell at the Siege of Louisburg, died at Cape Breton in 1745 (see *Catalogue of the Relics and Curiosities in Ye Olde Gaol, York, Maine*).

In contrast to the unusual Bulman bed hangings, the examples from the Massachusetts area form a more homogeneous, evolving group. The wide bed curtain thought to be associated with the Lowell family is clearly a Jacobean relative—one that has lost weight. Its hillock and sprawling three trunks are old subjects. The curling leaves have relaxed, but there is still a bit of eccentricity in the drawing of flowers and foliage. It is important, too, that the composition remains picturelike.

The design of the bed hangings that belonged to another prominent Boston family, the Bradstreets (but not to Anne, the poet, and her husband, Simon, who was an important magistrate— the needleworks came after their period), is different from the Bulman curtains, although the probable dates are the same, 1725–50. In the Bradstreet set the stems—they can no longer be called tree trunks—are slight and undulate gently upward, with little horizontal movement to distract from the vertical orientation. The flowers and leaves are comparatively naturalistic, and there is little abnormal curling. The predominant stitch in the bed furnishings and the seat covers made to accompany them is flat stitch.

A set of embroideries associated with Thomas Hancock (1703–64), a Boston merchant (and the uncle of John Hancock, who, in time, inherited it), includes valances, two head curtains, a headcloth, a coverlet with bases, and separate bases. The coverlet ap-

Bradstreet family bed curtains. Wool on cotton and linen. New England, 1725–50. Museum of Fine Arts, Boston, gift of Samuel Bradstreet.

Bradstreet family chair-seat covers, 1725–50. Museum of Fine Arts, Boston, gift of Samuel Bradstreet.

Bedcover. Thomas Hancock family. Wool on linen. 1725–50. Henry Francis du Pont Winterthur Museum.

pears quite different in design and much more refined than the other parts of the group, which have wide-spreading sprays with a few flowers and leaves. The headcloth has a rather linear Tree of Life, at the top of which is poised a bird. The coverlet is architectural in design and very exact in the drawing. The most striking element in the composition is a graceful tape trellis, very precisely designed. Through its columns flowering stems twine; its scrolls are elaborated with floral sprays. A highly conventionalized, neat border defines the center rectangle of the coverlet. The outer edge is bordered with nicely related, carefully proportioned sprays. The attached bases are scalloped in the same manner as those of the Bulman coverlet.

One's initial reaction to the Hancock cover is to wonder if it really was made in America. It is far more orderly and formal in design than most other embroidery of its period, although not the Bradstreet and Lowell pieces. On closer inspection, it is witty and surprising, as many American needleworks are. At the tops of its columns there are, instead of finials, two bending oak trees. At the center point between a pair of scrolls—a spot usually reserved for an urn by cabinetmakers using this device—stand three stately, if small and spiny, trees. The taped trellis is, in fact, very similar in design to looking-glass frames of the period. And the trees and flowers in this needlework are comparable to designs on petticoats, silk-emboidered workboxes, and looking-glass frames made in England, although these pieces customarily had a more informal, scattered arrangement or else a *horror vacui* composition.

All these bed furnishings, with the exception of the Bulman needleworks, came from the coastal area around Boston, where contact with England was close. The similarity of the motifs is intriguing. No pattern books have been found to suggest that books were the common source. It seems more likely that certain shops repeatedly sold the same or similar designs. Some are found on both English and American work. There is a parrot on the Bradstreet chair seat covers that appears on a wide curtain at the Museum of Fine Arts, Boston; also on an English bodice in the collection of the Victoria and Albert Museum, London; a heavily embroidered Jacobean bed curtain in the collection of the Embroiderers' Guild, London; and a piece (probably a chair seat) owned by the National Gallery, Washington, D.C. Though the colors vary slightly and the position is reversed at times, the designs of all are unmistakably from the same source.

Even more familiar and in more widespread use were the running dogs, stags, leopards, rabbits, and squirrels represented on

Bed curtain made by Sarah Noyes
Chester. Wethersfield, ca. 1740.
Wool on linen. Metropolitan
Museum of Art, gift of Mr. and Mrs.
Frank Coit Johnson, through their
son and daughter, 1944.

Fragment of a bedcover made by
Annie Warner, New England,
1750–75. Museum of Fine Arts,
Boston, gift of Mrs. Henrietta Page.

Bedcover made from bed curtains
and valances signed by Mary Breed.
Boston, 1770. Metropolitan Museum
of Art, Rogers Fund, 1922.

both sides of the Atlantic. These motifs are found not only in surface embroidery, but just as often in thread-counted work. Despite their common prototypes, the needleworks are different in significant ways. As Anne Rowe expresses it: "They . . . reach out from anonymity."

Connecticut embroideries are a reminder that this colony was spiritually and economically unlike Massachusetts. It was agricultural, comparatively isolated, and unadulterated in its Puritanism. Some products of the girls' schools—pictures, screens, seat covers, table covers—are not in evidence. Bed hangings made by Sarah Noyes Chester in Wethersfield around 1740 demonstrate the differences from the Bay Colony. The flowers are simple and more open, some of the stems are broad and have patterned fillings, and the flowers and leaves are drawn in a characteristic scriptlike manner in which groups of scallops are interrupted at intervals by a deep *U*, or round scallops alternate with points. The designs appear to be somewhat more conventionalized, but this is due in part to their open, linear treatment. As in Massachusetts, scrolling borders and scattered motifs were used.

It is tempting to try to correlate these embroideries with the pile-embroidered bed rugs (or coverlets) made in the area. In over-

Tree from the Mary Breed bedspread. The original was embroidered in predominantly pink, yellow, blue, and green shades, with Roumanian couching and herringbone, stem, buttonhole, and darning stitches.

all composition there is little similarity, but in the motifs more likeness can be found. Both use the cross-over stem and favor carnations and roses of a certain pattern, and in both a distinctive type of long serrated leaf can be found.

At mid-century embroidery with crewels changed. The heavier styles of furniture, Queen Anne and William and Mary, were being replaced by Chippendale. Needleworks made at the time have an uncertain quality about them; the designs are sometimes oddly erratic. But there also is a group that is very handsome and original. Some of the curtains are ornamented only with wide borders. The colors tend to be either monochrome blue or bright polychrome hues, and the drawing is very spare, giving the pieces a Persian air. A fragment by Annie Warner, made in New England between 1750 and 1775, is a fine example of American elegance without pretentiousness.

Another prime example of authentic American design is the needlework by Mary Breed, now a coverlet, but originally two curtains and three valances. Imagination is required to see the pieces as they once must have looked, but the individual tree motifs and the baskets and vases of flowers remain fresh and interesting. The embroidery was worked in polychrome crewels, primarily in flat stitch, on a linen and cotton ground of plain weave. Many of the

A second tree in the Breed spread is fancifully angular.

Tree design by the author liberally
adapted from trees in the Mary
Breed bedspread.

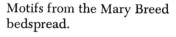

embroideries of the period are characterized by simple stitching. The Breed embroidery includes, in addition to flat stitch, button-holed fillings, couching, stem, outline, herringbone, and other stitches. Its color scheme is also unusual in containing a great deal of dark color.

There is no information about the maker of this important needlework other than that she was nineteen when she inscribed her work in 1770 and lived on Breed's Hill, actual site of the battle history has ascribed to nearby Bunker Hill.

Also belonging to this period is a delicately romantic pair of curtains with flowering vines and birds arranged in different ways. Two well-defined vines spring from a common source at the base of each composition. They form two wide borders that fill the space. The design sparkles with bright stylized flowers and lively birds.

With the coming of the Revolution embroidery with surface stitches in crewels went into decline. The old tradition did not revive after the war. Other forms took its place.

Wool-embroidered linen panels,
1750–1800. Henry Francis du Pont
Winterthur Museum.

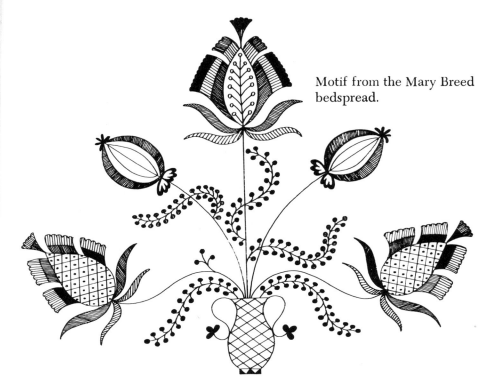

Motif from the Mary Breed bedspread.

One of the types of bedcovers that had been made before the war (an example in the Henry Ford Museum is dated ca. 1770), but was much more prevalent afterward, was the woolen blanket embroidered in surface stitches with heavy crewels. Many covers of this type were shaped and fringed; they were intended as bedspreads. Some were woven with widely spaced, narrow plaids. Embroidered designs were worked into the intervening spaces. Plain grounds usually were decorated with free-ranging vines, baskets of flowers reminiscent of the Tree of Life, and wavy or scalloped borders. The motifs were simplified and conventionalized, but they are within the tradition of earlier floral motifs, and many had embroidered dots.

The usual ground was either white or black. Fringes were a contrasting color. A variety of stitches were used, but the effect was open and linear.

An example from the Henry Ford Museum and dated 1778 comes from New York. It is of cream-colored homespun wool with small motifs worked within its squares. Rose, tulip, and bird are bare-bones versions of old motifs, as are the unusual feathered squares. The hearts are much like the more elaborate coverlet made by Hannah Pearl in the Pomfret-Hampton area of Connecticut during the same period (see page 136). Yarns for embroidery and fringe were dyed with indigo.

An earlier cover, made by Harriet (or Hannah) Dunbar of Lenox, Massachusetts, in 1760, is a superb example of a type of

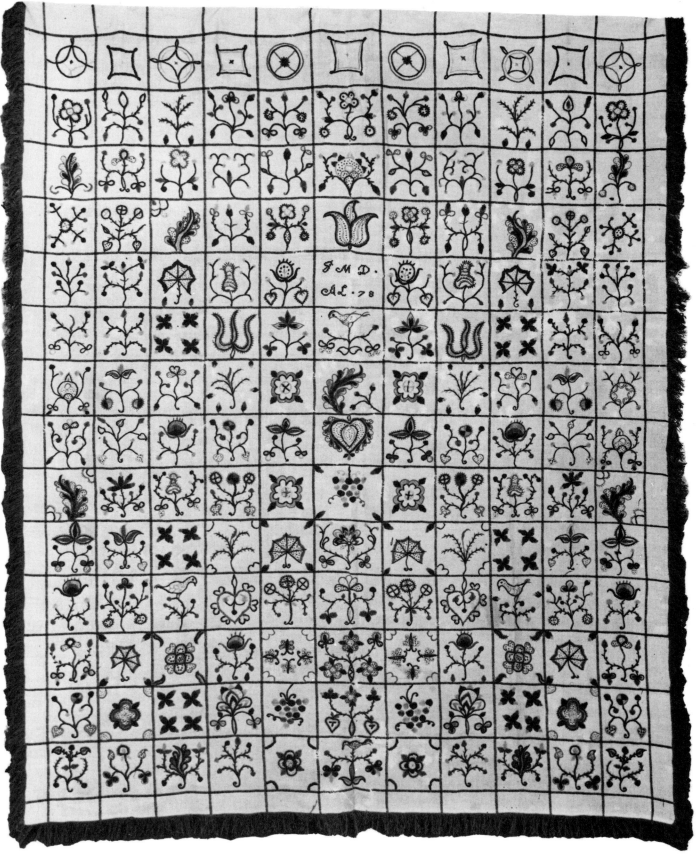

Bedcover inscribed S (?) M D./
A L. 78. Wool embroidery on wool.
New York, 1778. Greenfield Village
and Henry Ford Museum.

Wool embroidered linen seat cover. Connecticut, 1717. Art Institute of Chicago, gift of Mrs. Edna F. Wheeler.

layout that is still used today. It has a large central basket of flowers which is extended vertically, and unnaturally, so that it gives the effect of the Tree of Life, although its branches are much more willowy and less formal than those usually associated with that motif. The ground was assembled from five breadths of cloth. Apparently the loom used to make the black twill-woven cloth produced 23½-inch widths; three of these are used, plus two 5½-inch strips. The finished cover measures 88 by 81 inches.

To embroider the flower basket and the borders—made up of scallops plus stars topped by an assortment of individual floral motifs—a variety of stitches were used: blanket (open buttonhole), chain, detached chain, herringbone, outline, Roman, Roumanian, star, and surface satin, along with cut pile made with running stitch, an important American technique. The thread was two-ply crewel except for the flower centers, which were worked with the multiplied threads used to form these pile-embroidered segments. The colors of this coverlet are striking: peach, rose, red, leaf green, olive green, yellow, light blue, and light brown.

Quite similar, but without pile-embroidered areas, is the cover made in 1790 by the sisters of the Honorable Amos Patterson. It is a charming example of open working of flat stitching. Stem and herringbone stitches were used to make its wavy stems. With less

Space-filling pattern for embroidery derived from the chair seat on page 108. The original was worked in stroke stitch and long and short stitch, completely covering background and motifs.

open area and with stems embroidered in colors that contrast sharply with the background, its design has a more restless, vigorous appearance than the Dunbar cover, but its motifs are less varied. Colors are similar. The tassels of the Patterson coverlet are a whimsical touch, emboidered between scallops that, inexplicably, are not the same on both sides.

During the same years another type of bedcover was being made. These covers, now called bed rugs, were an art of the Connecticut River Valley primarily. The category includes all coverlets with embroidery entirely covering the surface. Some of the examples were worked with flat stitching, but most have pile embroidery. Thus, some of the pieces rightfully belong in the group now being considered, but because they have much in common with pile-surfaced bed rugs, a major achievement in the needlework of this country, they are included with those bedcovers.

In addition to bed furnishings American inventories of the late 1600s listed chair cushions (squabs) and cupboard covers. Gradually, upholstered furniture began to be used, and the idea of matching all the fabrics in a room began to gain favor.

Needlework was highly valued; it was carefully listed in inventories and wills. Its day-to-day treatment comes to light in a letter Chippendale wrote to a client suggesting that, in a room he

Coverlet made by Harriet (or Hannah) Dunbar, 1760. Wadsworth Atheneum.

Coverlet made by the sisters of the
Honorable Amos Patterson. Wool
embroidery on wool. New York,
about 1790. Art Institute of Chicago,
gift of the Needlework and Textile
Guild.

Part of an embroidered linen skirt. Ca. 1770. Metropolitan Museum of Art, gift of Elizabeth Haynes, 1972.

Wedding dress of Mary Myers Johnson. 1732. Wadsworth Atheneum, gift of Miss Emma S. Babcock.

was decorating with India paper, striped cotton slipcovers might be a good choice for the chairs. He added that the covers would give the chairs a finished look for the present and be "very necessary when cover'd with needlework."

Many small decorative items were embroidered. Fire screens, usually made in thread-counted embroidery, sometimes were surface stitched. Wall pockets, pincushions, and pot holders were also worked.

Crewel-Embroidered Clothing

In Connecticut wedding dresses were embroidered with crewels. The Wadsworth Atheneum, in Hartford, has a charming gown (not complete), made in 1732. The waist and skirt panel were made, according to family traditions, by Mary Meyers Johnson, who spun the thread, wove the linen cloth, and then embroidered it. The wool embroidery consists of flat filling stitches, stem stitch, and some surface darning.

The Metropolitan Museum has a similar skirt in undyed tabby-woven linen. Like the Hartford example, it is decorated with vining floral designs. Mary Meyers's wedding dress has undulating stems arranged vertically, but stopping short of the waistline. The sturdy flowering stems are studded with bright flowers, as are the sleeves. The scale of the embroidery on the bodice, appropriately, is smaller. The dress invites comparison with the Abigail Wadsworth gown, also a mid-eighteenth-century Connecticut creation, but embroidered in silk, rather than wool, and having spot motifs of a distinctly Connecticut type, rather than the flowering vine, which is also characteristic of other New England patterns.

Embroidered Rugs

A number of richly designed embroidered carpets survive. Among these the best known is the large (12-by-13½-foot) Caswell carpet. The project was the work of Zeruah Higley Guernsey, of Castleton, Vermont, with assistance from her family. The wool was spun by the members of the household, and Zeruah's father, who made spinning wheels and other mechanisms, furnished the needle. Ac-

cording to family lore, preserved by Mary Gerrish Higley, the carpet was made in a tambour frame, the work requiring about two or three years to finish. The stitch used for the carpet was called Kensington stitch by Zeruah; today it is known as chain stitch.

The carpet was made in square segments, each with a different design. The ground cloth is black. The embroidery yarn was dyed in shades of brown, blue, pink, yellow, red, green, and white.

The motifs include flowers, foliage, fruit, birds, butterflies, a rooster, dogs, cats, and humans. In one square the figures of a man and a woman were embroidered, then covered with another design. Two initialed squares are said to be the work of young Indians who were attending Castleton Medical College and staying with various families in town while they went to school. An unusual feature of

Rug made by Zeruah Higley Guernsey (later Caswell). Wool embroidery on wool in chain stitch. Castleton, Vermont, ca. 1832–35. Metropolitan Museum of Art, gift of Katherine Keyes, 1938, in memory of her father, Homer Eaton Keyes.

114

Stylized floral motifs inspired by
designs used in bed hangings and
other New England embroideries
of the second half of the eighteenth
century, sometimes worked entirely
in shades of blue.

Design for a chain-stitched rug.

Cartoon for the chain-stitched rug.

Wash bag of crewels on fustian.
England or America, 1712. Art
Institute of Chicago, restricted gift
of Miss Mildred Davison in honor
of Mrs. John V. Farwell III.

116 Petticoat border said to have been made by Mary Jones, Ipswich, Massachusetts, 1758. Museum of Fine Arts, Boston, Special Textile Fund.

the rug is a removable section of four squares that was basted into place in front of the hearth during the summer but removed when the fireplace was in use.

Zeruah Guernsey became Mrs. Caswell in 1846, and she lived in Castleton into old age. The carpet was kept on her parlor floor, but few people ever walked on it.

The design of the carpet is transitional. Some of the motifs are conventionalized in the manner of the eighteenth century; others have the large-scaled, full-blown feeling of the nineteenth. The use of the black background, which throws the motifs into sharp relief, is a nineteenth-century feature.

The idea of making embroidered carpets may have originated with the Pennsylvania Germans. Some thread-counted examples (see the chapter on "Thread-Counted Embroidery") have motifs exactly like those on Pennsylvania German show towels. Embroidered carpets were made in Germany from the fifteenth century. They also were made in England and Spain, where chain stitch was used.

The fine embroidered hearth rug, 29 by 59 inches, made by Jane Naomi Strong (Plate 3) is worked in stroke stitch, thread-counted throughout the background. This is a simple diagonal stitch in which the passage of thread on the back of the work is minimal and at right angles to the direction of the line of stitching.

Altar cloth made in the 1850s or 1860s by the grandmother of Mrs. Martínez Mullins, Santa Fe, New Mexico, as part of the furnishings for a chapel built by José Dolores Durán, Mrs. Mullins's grandfather. Embroidery in natural-dyed two-ply Saxony yarn in *colcha* stitch on commercial cotton drill. Collections of the Museum of New Mexico. Photograph by Arthur Olivas.

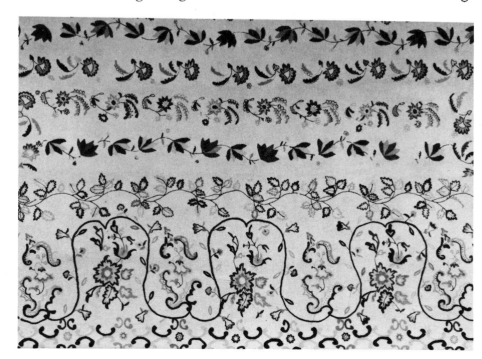

Petticoat border said to have been made by Miss Tabitha Lincoln (1728–1819). Wool embroidery on linen. New England, 1725–75. Museum of Fine Arts, Boston, gift of Frank Luscombe Tinkham.

The rows are closely set, so that none of the linen ground shows. Textile experts Cora Ginsburg and J. Herbert Callister, curator of textiles and costumes at the Wadsworth Atheneum, have determined that most of the tightly plied woolen yarns are single, S-plied, then doubled and Z-plied. In some areas, such as the leaf and cornucopia designs, heavier yarns were used. When Jane Strong's rug was exhibited in Hartford in 1829, it received the following commendation:

> This is to certify that Misses E. Hastings and J. Strong of the Town of Hartford have this day exhibited to the Hartford County Agricultural Society for Promoting Agriculture and Domestic Manufactures the Two Hearth Rugs considered extra meritorious for which they have received the Society's Premium, being a Bank Note worth One Dollar. May this evidence of merit stimulate them and their neighbors at the ensuing Anniversary. Hartford, October 7th, 1829. Harvey Seymour, Sect^y. Martin Kellog, Pres^t.

The rug is still a Hartford family affair. Miss Mary Todd, who gave the rug to the Atheneum, is the great-granddaughter of Jane Strong.

Colcha Embroidery of the Southwest

A group of distinctive embroidered panels, thought to be about a hundred years old, have been found in the Southwest, most of them in northeastern New Mexico and southeastern Colorado. It is believed that they were the work of craftsmen attached to wealthy haciendas. Some of the pieces are completely surfaced with woolen embroidery. These were worked on a tabby-woven cloth of merino, called *sabanilla*. They were used, it is thought, as table covers and rugs. Other panels were worked in open designs in wool on mantas twill woven of cotton or linen. The stitch used, called *colcha*, is a self-couched stitch, with quite short tying stitches laid at a forty-five-degree angle. The direction of the couching stitch reverses in each row, suggesting that two threads were used.

The dyes used in old *colcha* embroidery were produced from vegetable matter. The sap of the brazilwood tree was used for rose shades and brown. Reds also could be made from wild cherries, or they could be boiled out of bayeta cloth or made from cochineal, which had to be imported. Blossoms of chamiso, pale amarillo, and

118

Embroidered panel. Family of Mrs. Chávez of Capulin (San Luis Valley), Colorado. Hand-spun wool in *colcha* stitch worked solidly over hand-spun wool *sabanilla*. Red, indigo, yellow, green, and rosy-brown natural dyes. 1800–60. Collections of the Spanish Colonial Arts Society, at the Museum of New Mexico, gift of Mary Cabot Wheelwright. Photograph by Arthur Olivas.

canaigre gave yellows. Blues were made from indigo; sumac produced blacks and some browns.

There is no firm evidence on how these needleworks came to be made in the Southwest. Some believe that laid-stitch needleworks imported from the Orient for use in the churches in Mexico, and later brought to the United States, may have suggested the method that was used for the *colchas*. Others see in them Spanish Moorish traits, which also could have arrived via Mexico. Still others cite the subject matter (domestic and fantastic animals, birds, blossoms and sprigs, baskets and vases) as proof that they derived from New England. Yet the formality of the compositions is not typical of New England. The pieces entirely surfaced with woolen embroidery have designs unlike anything in the East, designs more related to weaving than to other embroidery. Often they are striped with stylized floral patterns or repeated geometric figures.

The designs made in the 1840s were checked or had small flowers. In the 1860s and 1870s striped patterns were worked. All the compositions are extremely simple. Many have heavy, vertical zigzagged bands, perhaps softened by scalloping the contour. Sometimes a diapered pattern was used. One bedcover has a simple, formal, three-blossomed sprig in the center of each lozenge. Unlike most embroidery in crewels, the design remains the same in each compartment in these works of the Southwest.

A number of *colchas* have white grounds with the central section divided into bold panels. One has three red sections alternating with white. Against this ground are arranged slender laurel leaves and stems in green, dark when against the lighter ground, light when against red.

Scrolls do not occur so frequently as in New England embroidery, but one example has a complicated design of Spanish flavor carefully worked in red, green, white, and smaller amounts of yellow and black.

Samplers in Woolen Surface Embroidery

Although a few samplers with woolen surface stitching can be found, most samplers are thread-counted embroidery in either silk or wool, surface stitching in silk, or a combination of thread-counting and surface stitching. However, among the emboideries of the Southwest are some extraordinary compositions worked in cotton, one of which, at least, can be called a sampler. It is presumed that these works came from northern New Mexico, probably near Santa

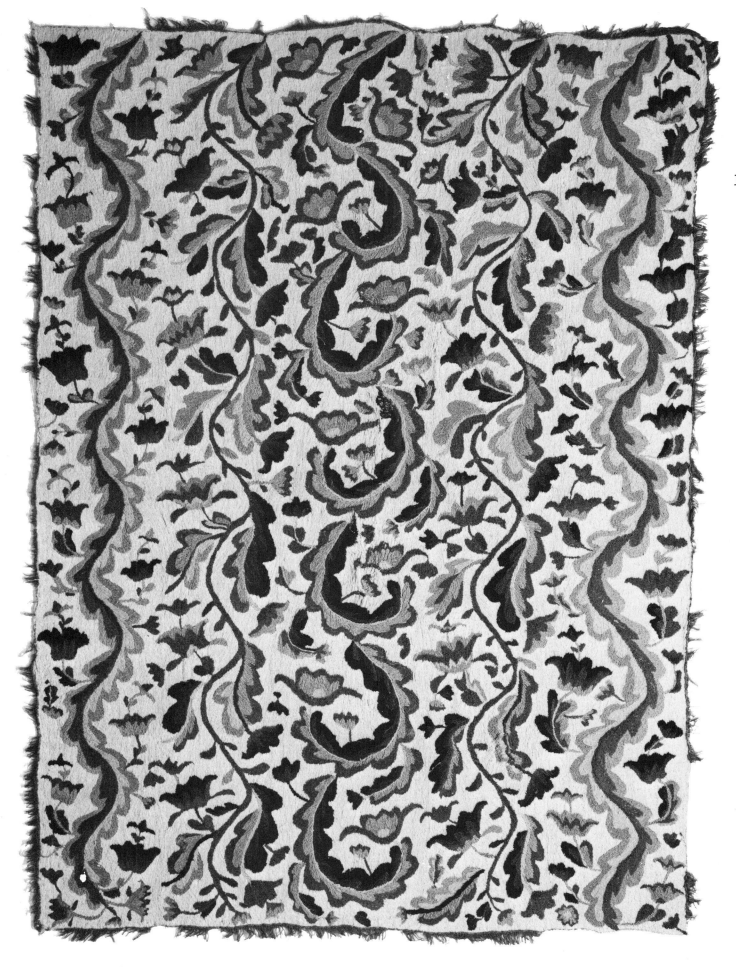

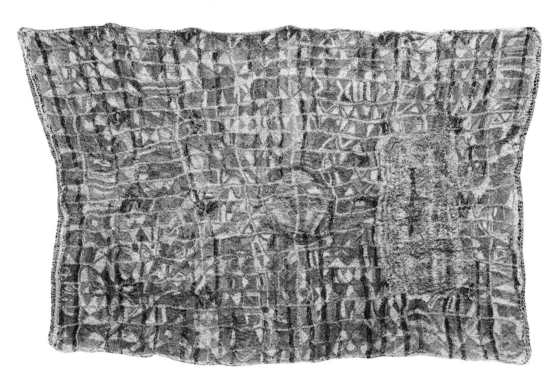

Panel by Policarpio Valencia. Cotton carpet warp in buttonhole stitch on a hand-woven blanket. Collections of the Museum of New Mexico. Photograph by Arthur Olivas.

Cruz in the Rio Grande valley. They are large and made of humble materials, with an extremely interesting choice of stitches. The work was done mainly in buttonhole stitch, the stitch of needle lace, and the compositions have all the characteristics of contemporary needle lace, although they were worked on a ground. Buttonhole stitch was used in a variety of colors for filling, outlining, background, and edging.

In three pieces on which the name Policarpio Valencia is inscribed, buttonhole stitch is the only stitch used. One is a panel made on an old hand-woven Rio Grande blanket of hand-spun wool patterned in horizontal stripes with several rows of hollow diamonds in brown and pink on white. The cotton carpet-warp (string) embroidery has faded, but it originally probably was white, blue, red, orange, brown, and lemon yellow. An inscription on the reverse reads, as translated,

If this treasure should be lost, as
It is wont to happen, I entreat the one who finds
It he must give it back to me, and if he should be
Long of fingernails and short of understanding
I beg him to be mindful of the
Seventh commandment. That is all.

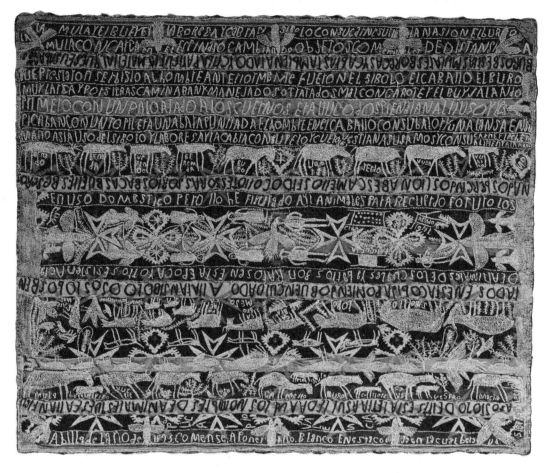

Another embroidery, less detailed in stitching, but clearer in design, has a lengthy inscription in buttonhole stitch made with blue and white four-ply cotton string and other indistinct bits of faded color. The base is a commercially woven weft twill cloth with cotton warp and woolen wefts forming a double face. Predominantly dark gray, the cloth has weft stripes of red, black, light gray, green, and yellow. The design of the embroidery was planned to make use of the striped ground.

Almost by accident it was learned that Valencia was a long-time resident of Santa Cruz whose emboidery, weaving, rug hooking, and woodworking were familiar in his area. In 1950 Irene Emery, as honorary associate in textiles for the School of American Research, analyzed three of his pieces. Her work, which included the identification of the artist, later was published in *El Palacio*, a monthly review of the arts and sciences of the Southwest (see Irene Emery, "Samplers Embroidered in String," *El Palacio*, February 1953). Since all the known pieces included lettering—two then known were almost completely covered with it—translations were of pressing interest. Letters faced in different directions, were confusing or indistinguishable, but a translation, the work of several people, finally was worked out, through the efforts of Dr. Kercheville, Dr. Cobos, and Dr. Pearce of the University of New Mexico;

Embroidery by Policarpio Valencia. Buttonhole stitch in cotton string on double-faced cotton and wool cloth. Santa Cruz, New Mexico, 1925. Collections of the Museum of New Mexico. Photograph by Arthur Olivas.

Analysis of a four-way symmetrical design to be found in *colcha* embroideries. The drawing is based on an example in the Museum of International Folk Art.

Mrs. Frances Urban of Santa Fe; Mrs. Stella Lucero of Santa Cruz; and various staff members and visitors at the Laboratory of Anthropology in Santa Fe. On the samplerlike embroidery included here, many of the lines of lettering simply identified the animals and tools that were shown, but the main body of lettering proves that Policarpio was something of a poet:

On April 2 of the year 1925 I began to work white thread onto this coverlet, on which you will see a certain collection of animals among which various ones are rare in these times and others still exist for domestic use, but I have sketched here animals to be remembered. Those that served mankind in times past were the buffalo the horse the donkey the mule and the ox and the sheep and goat; the buffalo with its meat sustained the people, the donkey [and] mule, beasts of burden, carrying loads on their backs, exchanging commercial goods over great distances and mountains, traveling slowly and driven brutally with a club and the ox pulling in front with a pole tied to his horns. This was a yoke: two oxen were bound to the yoke and they prodded them with a topil, a sharp pointed stick. The man on horseback with daring and with a spear in his hand made use of the buffalo and the sheep and the goat whose pelts and hides were used to clothe their masters and with whose meat and milk the people were fed.

The ambiguity of the placing of the lettering is only the least of the characteristics that make Policarpio a true son of the twentieth century. His completely nonobjective works, creatively more stimulating, but not so well preserved as this samplerlike piece, are astonishing when viewed in the context of work being made in the 1920s. Although he seems not to have had any formal training in art, he had extraordinary sensitivity. His work, to date little known, anticipated the spirit of individuality that prevails among embroiderers today.

Notes on technique

In colonial America crewels could be purchased in various grades. Women who lived in port cities could buy threads put up in skeins. Other women (those who lived in inland towns like Deerfield, Massachusetts, for example) made their threads themselves. The popularity of shaded effects in crewel surface embroidery has a practical as well as an aesthetic basis. One dye pot could yield a

"Sampler" by Policarpio Valencia.
Cotton buttonhole stitch on a
patchwork base of faded blue denim
and other cloth. Collections of the
Museum of New Mexico. Photograph by Arthur Olivas.

Bedspread made and signed by
Mercy Post, Newport, June 2, 1824.
Wool embroidery in tans and greens
on dark-blue wool twill. Art
Institute of Chicago, gift of
Minnie E. Post.

number of shades of a given hue, depending upon how long the thread was left in the bath or upon the strength of the bath, which weakened with each dye lot.

In England wool was the fiber used for the clothing and household furnishings of the lower classes; it was not expensive. Silk, which had to be imported from the Levant or the Orient until the seventeenth century, was quite costly. Wool was certainly an appropriate fiber for large-scale Jacobean designs, and it made warm bed curtains and other hangings. One wonders whether the English, who loved rich effects, might not have made those embroideries with silk if it had been more readily available. The early attempts at raising silkworms in England were not successful, and in America they were abandoned in favor of the more profitable crop of tobacco.

As noted earlier, a popular ground for embroidery with crewels was fustian, which is usually twill-woven with a linen warp and cotton weft, although some are velvet-woven or made entirely of cotton. An occasional bed curtain can be found that has its original napped surface; there is one at the Museum of Fine Arts, Boston.

Another ground, called dimity, was either all cotton or a cotton-linen blend a great deal like corduroy. Mixtures of cotton and linen are excellent for embroidery. Cotton is soft, and linen is stiff; the combination yields an excellent texture. In America, the most widely used ground was tabby-woven (plain-woven) linen, but it is possible to stitch more accurately on closely woven twills than on tabby weaves.

All cloth exported from England between 1774 and 1811 had three blue threads woven into the selvages, and the presence of these threads is helpful in dating a piece of needlework and in determining whether it is of English or American origin.

All tools were highly valued. Thimbles were made of brass, bone, silver, ivory, or gold. They were kept in special cases, which often were small works of art, in silver, bone, wood, tortoiseshell, and enamel. Needles were equally valued. Both round and square types were imported, but about mid-eighteenth century needles began to be manufactured in this country. Needles and pins were also kept in special cases fashioned of the same materials as those for thimbles.

Advertisements seldom mention embroidery frames, but beautiful frames of numerous types were used. The advertisements do, however, give some insights into the stocks that were available for embroiderers. In the *Pennsylvania Packet* of July 31, 1775, Nicholas Brooks, who dealt chiefly in silver, offered "best black pencils, best

Dutch wax and wafers, types for marking linens with coleurs and directions; silk waistcoat patterns, very elegant; assortment of pictures and maps, in books or single . . . India ink." It also was possible to buy linens with patterns already drawn on them, made either in England or America.

Colonial women used the same stitches employed in England for Jacobean and later woolen embroidery, but they tended to simplify technique, usually choosing stitches that were easily worked and that put most of the thread on the face of the work. The stitches most commonly employed for filling areas were either flat or self-couched stitches. Larry Salmon, curator of textiles at the Museum of Fine Arts, Boston, warns that both types of stitching have been identified as Roumanian stitch in the past; today only the latter is given that name.

Three line stitches were used by all embroiderers: crewel, stem, and outline. Crewel stitch has been identified as the same as stem stitch, but not so wide, an ambiguous definition of an illusive stitch. Stem stitch and outline stitch are the same, except that in making stem stitch the thread is worked to the right of the needle, while in outline, or true, stitch, it is kept to the left. To explain it another way, in stem stitch each successive stitch is above the last; in outline each successive stitch is below the last. Outline is slightly more awkward to work and produces the "truest" line, which is probably why it also is called true stitch.

Diagrams given below show some of the stitches to be found in surface stitching made with crewels. Most of the stitches also are employed in making silk embroidery, although certain stitches are used more with one thread than with the other.

There are differences between English and American embroidery that should be noted. Self-couching and flat stitching often are used in American embroidery in areas that in English work would be embroidered in long and short stitch. Dense satin-stitched brick designs and complicated laidwork are not typical of American work, nor are fancy fillings arranged from several different stitches.

Running Stitch. This sewing stitch is also used in surface and thread-counted embroidery. For double running stitch make spaces and stitches the same length, then work back in the opposite direction, completely filling all the spaces.

Back Stitch. Bring up the needle one stitch length beyond the start of the stitching line. Reinsert the needle at the start of the line and bring it up one stitch length beyond the point of the first insertion.

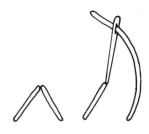

Arrowhead Stitch. For both stitches, insert the needle at the angle point.

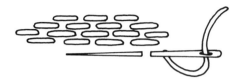

Darning Stitch. Make stitches all the same length, picking up only one or two threads of the ground. The embroidery thread used is usually heavier than that of the ground, to form a dense cover. Little thread appears on the back of the work.

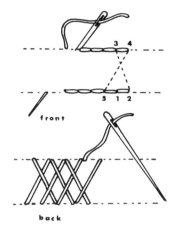

Crossed Back Stitch. Work between two guidelines in the numbered sequence shown on the diagram. Use this stitch on sheer fabric; the crosses will show through the cloth.

Stroke Stitch. Make slanting stitches, carrying the thread horizontally across the back of the work, as shown. Work stitches in closely packed rows.

Outline Stitch (Crewel Stitch). Make a short stitch that slants slightly upward. Bring up the thread for the second stitch below and a bit beyond the first stitch. Repeat.

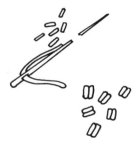

Seed Stitch (Speckling Stitch). Scatter small stitches or pairs of stitches over a design area to create a textured effect.

Herringbone Stitch. Work from left to right between guidelines. Slant a stitch from upper left to lower right and bring the needle up again a short distance to the left before slanting the next stitch to the right. Stitches can be widely or closely spaced.

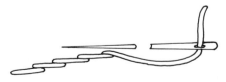

Stem Stitch. Working left to right along a drawn guideline, bring up the needle at the end of the line. Insert the needle one stitch length to right and slightly below the guideline. Bring up the needle for the second stitch slightly to the right and above the line. Repeat. Use as a line stitch, or work rows close together for filling.

Tied Herringbone Stitch. Work a second thread of a contrasting color across the row in CORAL STITCH, zigzagging between the thread crossings.

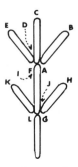

Fern Stitch. Make stitches as shown, following the sequence lettered on the diagram.

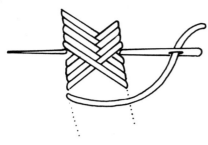

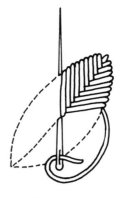

Basket Stitch. Work between guidelines. Beginning at the top left, bring the needle down and right at a forty-five-degree angle and insert. Bring the needle up directly opposite at the left. Then insert at the right, opposite the beginning of the work, making a large *X*. Bring the needle to the surface directly below the point at which the work started, and repeat.

Satin Stitch. Set parallel stitches close together to fill small motifs completely. Align stitch ends carefully. Satin stitch covers the back of the work as thoroughly as the front.

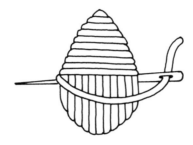

Padded (or Raised) Satin Stitch. Make a layer of SATIN STITCHES in one direction for padding; cover it with a second layer worked at right angles.

Fishbone Stitch. Draw a center rib through a small motif. Make a straight stitch at the top of the rib. Bring the needle up on the outer edge of the motif, a little to one side. Insert the needle on the center line and bring it up just under the first stitch, but this time on the opposite side of the motif. Insert the needle again on the center line, just below the second stitch. Repeat, alternating left and right.

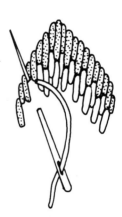

Flat Stitch. Lay a long stitch across the area to be worked. Bring the needle up again as close as possible to the end of the stitch and make a second stitch in the opposite direction, setting the stitches very close together. Repeat to fill the area. This looks very much like SATIN STITCH, but wastes little thread on the back of the work. Flat stitch can be radiated in a circle; the irregular edge and spreading stitches create a delicate effect.

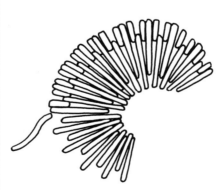

Wedge Stitch. Insert short stitches in the outer curve of circular or serpentine areas of FLAT STITCHING to fill out the embroidery.

Long and Short Stitch. Begin at the outer edge of the motif. Slant close-set, alternately long and short stitches toward an axis determined by the motif. Start the stitches in subsequent rows at the points where those of the previous row end. For subtly shaded effects use different shades or contrasting colors for each new row.

128

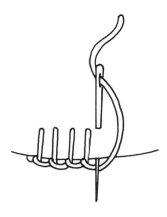

Buttonhole Stitch. Insert the needle above the stitch line. Bring it to the surface on the line, keeping the working thread under the needle. Repeat. Stitch spacing and length are a matter of choice. BLANKET STITCH is a widely spaced buttonhole stitch.

Long and Short Buttonhole Stitch. Work BUTTONHOLE STITCHES, spacing them out, in alternating lengths.

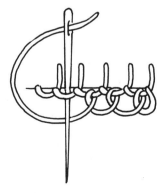

Detached Buttonhole Stitch. Work a row of BUTTONHOLE or CHAIN STITCHES. Work back over the row in buttonhole stitch, engaging only the stitches of the previous row and not the ground fabric. Repeat in the opposite direction for the desired number of rows. This stitch is the basis of most needle lace stitches.

Buttonholed Wheel. Work BUTTONHOLE STITCHES of even length around a central point. Tightly pulled stitches will produce an eyelet.

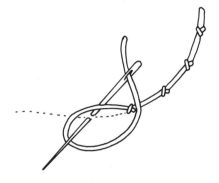

Coral Stitch. Bring the thread up at the start of the design line. Hold the thread on the line with your free thumb. Make a short diagonal stitch under the thread. Draw the needle through with the thread looped under it. Space knots as desired. Stitches can be zigzagged or worked along curves.

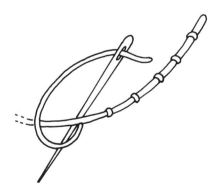

Couching. Secure one or more decorative threads to the fabric by means of a separate (and usually finer) thread. Insert the couching thread at right angles to the laid thread. Make tiny straight stitches and draw them up tight. The tying stitches may be arranged to form patterns, from simple stripes and checks to intricate geometrics and floral forms.

129

Padded Couching. Lay a padding of couched, flat, or satin stitches at right angles to the direction in which the overlying couched work will run, then add couching as above.

Roumanian Couching (Self-Couching). Lay a long stitch across the area to be couched (or tied). With the same needle and thread, work back across it making long, slack tying stitches that leave very little thread on the back. Repeat, laying stitches close together to fill the design area.

Roumanian Stitch. This is the same as ROUMANIAN COUCHING, except that the laid stitches are shorter, and only one slanting stitch is required to tie. It is also called overlaid, universal, New England, American, economy, and other names, and when used as a filling stitch, self-couching.

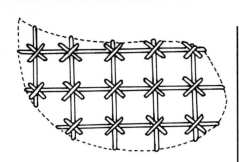

Trellis Couching. Lay long, equally spaced parallel stitches vertically and horizontally across the design area. Make small cross stitches across each intersection to secure the laid threads.

Straight Overcast Stitch. Make tiny stitches close together at right angles to the design line. You may first lay down a line of running stitches to use as padding. For DIAGONAL OVERCAST STITCH slant the stitches.

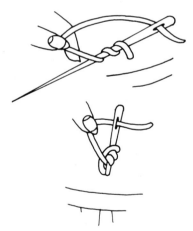

French Knot. Bring the thread to the surface. Holding it taut with your free hand, twist it one or more times around the needle. Maintaining firm tension, insert the needle one thread away from the point where it emerged, and pull it through the fabric, keeping a tight hold on the thread with the other hand, so that a compact knot is formed. The fabric should be held firm in a hoop or stretcher; it is not easy to work French knot on a slack surface.

Rope Stitch. Working along a guideline, bring the thread up a little below the line and insert the needle again a little farther on. Bring it to the surface just beyond the starting point, twist the thread around as for FRENCH KNOT, and pull the thread and needle through the twist. Place these diagonal stitches close together to produce a ropelike appearance.

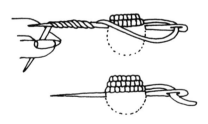

Bullion Stitch. Use a needle with an eye that does not bulge. Bring the thread to the surface at the left end of the stitch to be made. Insert the needle at the right end of the stitch, pushing it through to only about half its length, and bring the point up again at left. With the thread held taut in your left hand, twist the thread several times around the needle. Hold the twists back with your thumb and bring the needle and thread through the twists. Pull the needle and twisted thread back to the right, tightening the working thread to hold the twists in position, and insert the needle down through the fabric to complete the stitch.

Chain Stitch. Bring the thread to the surface. Holding the thread with the opposite thumb, insert the needle at the starting point. Bring it to the surface one stitch length farther along the design line, keeping the thread under the needle. Repeat, inserting the needle next to the point where it last emerged.

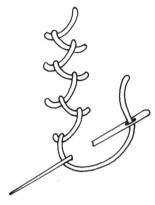

Feather Stitch may be made along a center guideline or (for uniformity) between two parallel guidelines or wander at random in free stitchery. When working along a single line (as to cover the seams between quilt patches), bring the thread to the surface slightly below the top and to the left of the line. To make the first stitch, insert the needle just opposite the top end of the line and slightly to the right. Bring it up again lower down and to the left of the line, holding the thread under the needle. Repeat, inserting the thread at the right again, below the first stitch, or vary the stitch by alternating the starting point of each stitch from left to right. For CRETAN STITCH follow the same procedure but make wide stitches, closely spaced.

Coverlet initialed A L and dated
1832. Wool on wool. Greenfield
Village and Henry Ford Museum.

III Bed Rugs and Pile Embroidery

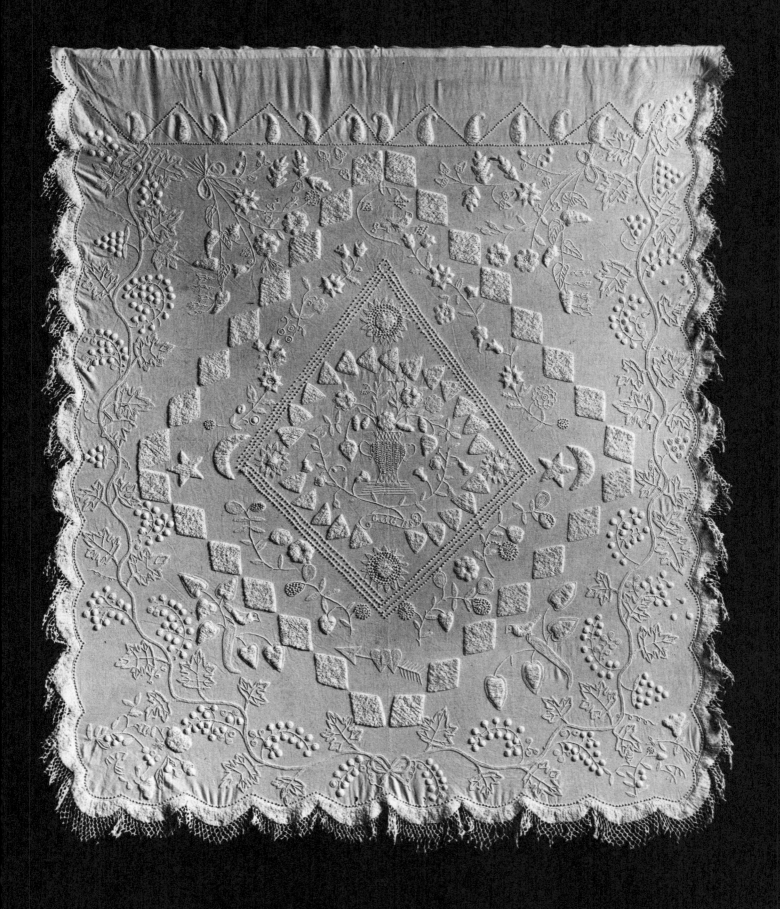

Bed Rugs and Pile Embroidery

A "rug," in the seventeenth century, was a heavy cover for a bed. Later, after the word began to be used for floor coverings as well, the covers were called bed rugs—a term not unknown in earlier years, but one not frequently used until 1922, when it gained currency in *Antiques* magazine. In an edition of John Fletcher's play *The Night-Walker, or The Little Theife* printed in 1640 we read: "I wished 'em then get him to bed, and they did so, and almost smother'd him with rugges and pillowes." In the same vein the Reverend Nathaniel Ward of Ipswich, Massachusetts, wrote in *The Simple Cobbler of Aggawam* in 1647: "To speak to light heads with heavy words, were to break their necks; to cloathe Summer matter, with Winter Rugge, would make the Reader sweat."

The exceptional rug was the one used on the floor. In *Bed Ruggs/1722–1833* William L. Warren and J. Herbert Callister note in the 1684 inventory of Joseph Winn, a Roxbury butcher, a listing of "a small feet rug," but what type of rug this was is unclear.

Floor coverings, rare in America, were called carpets or carpits (there were several spellings). Usually carpets were used for tables or cupboards rather than on floors. On the Continent and in England, Oriental carpets were known and admired from early times, but they did not come into use in England until the sixteenth century, probably because of the difficulty and length of the journey from the Near East. Finally Henry VIII acquired some Turkish carpets for Hampton Court. The rich colors and geometric medallions of these works of art are familiar through the paintings of Hans Holbein.

In England weavers made their own versions of the carpets of the Orient. Knotting patterns into their weaving, they created Turkey work, which was popular in the sixteenth century. Inventories indicate that there was Turkey work in America as well before 1670, but styles lagged a bit in the colonies, and it apparently continued in vogue among colonists until about 1758, after it had gone out of fashion elsewhere. Turkey work was used for cushion covers and for furniture carpets. Colonel Francis Epes and John

Coverlet initialed C A C 1859. Running stitch with cut pile, stem stitch, satin stitch, and French knots on tabby-woven cotton foundation, two breadths seamed vertically. Knotted fringe. Probably Vermont. Wadsworth Atheneum, gift of William L. Warren.

136 Bed rug made by Hannah Pearl. Wool stem-stitch embroidery on natural wool foundation. Connecticut, Pomfret-Hampton area. Wadsworth Atheneum. Lent by Miss Isabel Rogers, Boston.

Carter of Virginia had chairs upholstered in Turkey work, as did Richard Phillips of South Carolina. A Turkey-work chair seat was twice as valuable as a leather seat. The most popular colors seem to have been red, brown, buff, blue, green, black, and magenta. Along with dark wood, polished silver, and blue delftware, the colorful geometric patterns must have created a rich effect.

Seventeenth-century American probate records include the terms carpet, coverlet, and rug, each in various spellings. Realizing that most houses at the time had bare floors, except perhaps for a covering of rushes or a braided or woven mat, we must understand "carpet" as meaning a table cover or runner, cupboard cloth, or perhaps chair seat. A coverlet could be any outer covering for the bed; a rug was a coverlet whose surface was completely covered with either flat or pile embroidery. As suggested in *Bed Ruggs/1722–1833*, they must have been folded at the foot of the bed when not needed.

William L. Warren, while director of the Litchfield Historical Society, became interested in the pile bedcovers of the Connecticut River Valley area. He had been researching them for five years when in 1967 J. Herbert Callister began to explore the possibility of an exhibition of bed rugs at the Wadsworth Atheneum, Hartford, Connecticut. The showing, held in 1972, provided for the first time an opportunity for comparison of the known examples.

Gertrude Townsend, fellow for research at the Museum of Fine Arts, Boston, was quick to identify the technique as embroidery, rather than hooking, which it had previously been supposed to be. Long acquainted with the rugs through photographs, she recog-

Bed rug made by Rachel Packard.
Running stitch in wool. Jericho,
Vermont, 1805. Greenfield Village
and Henry Ford Museum, gift of
Mrs. Delia Borgers.

138 Value relationships in a bed rug in the collection of the Shelburne Museum. The motifs in the original are worked in running stitch in green, tans, and gold, with accents of brick red, on a brownish-black ground.

nized the method when Mr. Warren brought her some examples for inspection. On the face, the stitches appear to be hooked, but their position on the back clearly shows that a different method is involved. In hooking, the tool enters the ground fabric and returns via the same opening in the cloth, but in the embroidered rugs, loops were made with running stitches, the needle entering at one point and being brought back at another. All the pile rugs in the exhibition turned out to be embroidered. The combined research of the three scholars was published in the outstanding exhibition catalogue quoted above.

There is a precedent for the pile bed rug. (In fact the term is related to the Old Norwegian word rögg, which means tufts, or shagginess, and the dialect word rugga or rogga, which signifies a coarse coverlet.) Scandinavian colonists brought pile rugs to America at an early date, and in the seventeenth century they seem to have been commonplace. Originally such rugs were striped or plain, but a patterned version later evolved. These rugs, which had a pile added during weaving, are easily confused with embroidered pile rugs.

Wool was the usual foundation in making bed rugs, but an occasional linen ground is found. Heavy woolen yarn, as a rule composed of several plies, was used for the pile. Some of the foundations are a single wide piece of cloth; others are two, two and a half, or three widths sewn together. In some rugs the pile was cut; in others it was left uncut. And there are some that have both cut and uncut loops.

Sometimes one reads of a technique in which the loops were gauged by working them over a reed, and the stitches cut to release the reed. Actually, no special tool is really necessary in working the stitch. If the ground fabric is loosely woven, so that the threads do not drag against it, and if the needle is large, opening a good-sized hole, there is no problem in making the loops or in keeping them even in height. Pile that is to be uncut, of course, requires more care.

In England and Scotland rugs were commonly worked with short lengths of cloth or yarn called thrums, which were drawn through a cloth backing of loose weave, producing a dense pile. This technique, like hooking, can be confused with the embroidered pile technique.

Bed-rug patterns are akin to those of other surface embroidery, in the same way that designs of Oriental carpets and Turkey work relate to thread-counted stitching on canvas. In the Caucasus, where men wove carpets as women embroidered alongside them, both used the same patterns.

A major difference between hooking and pile embroidery lies in the fact that embroidery produces a more flexible, lighter object. Hooking, a mechanical technique, requires a stiffer ground to support loops that must be packed closely together so that they will not pull out easily. Most of the rugs shown here were made with wool threads on a tabby-woven wool foundation. Usually three breadths were seamed together vertically to make a large enough backing. Occasionally a fourth narrow strip was added to increase the breadth.

Another difference between hooked and embroidered rugs is the material used for the work. Bed rugs always were embroidered with new material of fine quality. Often the entire rug appears to be of home manufacture, from the raising of the wool or flax, through the spinning, weaving, and dyeing processes, to the embroidery. Hooking, a later craft, was frequently done with strips of cloth cut from discarded clothing, sometimes from fabrics that were commercially produced.

Turkey-work cushion. England, ca. 1650–60. Art Institute of Chicago, restricted gift of Florence Dibell Bartlett.

The question arises whether designs were handed down from mother to daughter in the same manner that produced the traditionalism of some European folk arts and, indeed, the quilts of the United States. There is an undeniable professionalism about the design of many of the bed rugs. The most common central motif is a vase of flowers or Tree of Life. Surrounding it is a coiling stem or vine, with a rose, carnation, or other flower within each coil. Some of the rugs contain only coiling flowering stems, arranged vertically.

The nearly identical designs of a number of the bed rugs obviously have a common source, but their variations are intriguing. Comparing the bed rugs, it is necessary to separate workmanship from drawing. Naturally, subtleties of drawing may be obscured by long pile or widely spaced stitching, but even in some rugs that are not very precisely made, refinements of design can be detected that suggest that some sensibility other than the maker's was at work in the planning. Also, the average amateur does not draw with the bold sweep that is characteristic of many of these rugs.

The evidence for the manner of transmitting designs is scanty. For example, J. Herbert Callister relates that Eunice Williams Metcalf of Lebanon, Connecticut, who embroidered a bed rug about 1790 or 1800, was, according to family genealogy, an aunt of Philena McCall, whose rug is shown in color in Plate 2. There is considerable similarity in design between the two. But Philena's rug is dated 1802, so it is equally possible that a third party may have designed the rugs for both Philena and her aunt. Moreover, the design of a rug in the Shelburne Museum is almost identical to the Philena McCall bed rug, except for the upturning vine ends at the top, but its execution is far less sophisticated. Contours were not kept so carefully. Shading is much less precise and definite. Some of the difference may be accounted for in the choice of a dark background for the Shelburne rug, but it really is the hands of the makers that are responsible for the greatest difference—the one rendition soft and full, the other tense and spare.

Even closer to the Philena McCall bedcover is one at the Metropolitan Museum of Art dated 1809 and initialed M B. It is worked in running stitch and cut pile on three breadths of tabby-woven fabric. Like the Shelburne cover, it has a dark ground, but its precise contours more nearly approach those of Philena McCall's rug.

Three earlier rugs, one definitely identified with Colchester, Connecticut, and the others presumed to have come from the area, were done with flat stitches instead of all-pile embroidery. The motifs were embroidered with thread-counted, pattern-darned

Bed rug initialed M B and dated
1809. Connecticut River Valley.
Metropolitan Museum of Art,
Rogers Fund, 1913.

142   Bed rug signed by Mary Foot.
Probably Connecticut, Colchester
area, dated 1778. Henry Francis
du Pont Winterthur Museum.

stitches in dark-colored yarn. Lighter colors were then worked into
the intervening spaces. Contours were worked with rows of light
and dark running stitches, the light rows next to the pattern-darned
filling. The background was worked entirely in running stitches.
The total effect is much like that of English blackwork, but on a
monumental scale.

Two of the pattern-darned rugs, possibly made as early as 1760,
belong to the group designed with a central tree with surrounding,
meandering vines (equivalent to the curling leaves of the McCall
rug and the Shelburne Museum's example). The third one, made by
Mary Foot in 1778 and pictured here, has a flowering bush within
a box. Its outer border is a flowering vine. The simplicity of the
motifs, the scale and spacing, suggest that this pattern could have
been the work of the same designer who made the Tree of Life
patterns.

Curiosity about the design process naturally arises. Patterned,
flat fillings of various sorts are also seen in block-printed lining
papers used for document boxes and trunks of the seventeenth
century. Whether the papers suggested designs for embroidery or
the embroidery suggested designs for papers is an unresolved question. Possibly designers of the period simply worked out patterns
for both. The box that contained the patent of Plymouth Colony,

Bed rug initialed N L. Running stitch with cut and uncut pile. Connecticut, dated 1796. Metropolitan Museum of Art, Rogers Fund, 1933.

made out to "Wm. Bradford and Associates," had a coarse pattern of this kind; its similarity to the design of the flat-stitched bed rugs is striking.

Two of the most beautiful pile-embroidered bed rugs are one made by Hannah Johnson in 1796 in Bozrah, New London County, Connecticut, when she was twenty-six years old (shown in color in Plate 4) and an example now in the Metropolitan Museum of Art in New York. The latter, marked N L, is dated the same year as Hannah Johnson's. The two rugs are so much alike that there can be little doubt that they are the work of the same designer. The ground of each is made up of three breadths of tabby-woven woolen cloth 27½ inches wide, plus a narrow strip. One wonders whether the patterns on these grounds could have been sketched by some itinerant artist or some unknown peddler who, like Edward Sands Frost, the designer of hooked rugs (see page 292), prepared his grounds at home during rainy weather. The possibility that a book or pattern might have been the common source seems less likely, because achieving fine drawing on large scale would have been a formidable task for most amateur artists, and most of the needlewomen of the time, although skilled in needlework technique, were not professional artists. A rug in almost an identical pattern was made in 1773 by Molly Stark, wife of General John Stark.

At Historic Deerfield there is a cut-down rug, dated 1790 and initialed E B, that also closely resembles these examples, except that its color scheme is different: shades of orange, olive, and dark green against a blue background. The others have natural grounds with shades of brown, tan, gold, and a few accents.

In all there are thirteen known bed rugs with similar patterns. Some are naïve enough to be homemade copies of other rugs. In nine the drawing is expert and the embroidery technique very accomplished. The bold hand that set the curves onto these large woolen grounds was a practiced one. The sameness of the motifs and their slight variations suggest that some workaday artist of superior talent acquainted with Eastern models might have sketched them freehand onto their grounds, some days making the reciprocating curves a bit smaller than on other days, sometimes making the vines into leaves. One has the impression of a busy artist content with the ubiquitous carnation and occasional rose, but finding endless variations within a limited vocabulary of motifs, although considering the long span over which the rugs were designed, there may have been more than one artist.

Candlewicking

Candlewicking is a technique related to the running-stitch embroidery of bed rugs. The difference is the open-spaced arrangement of the candlewicking in contrast to the entirely covered surfaces of the bed rugs. But it is related also to another technique. During the late seventeenth century English women made white linen bedspreads with clustered flowers and fruits and vines, using knotting, couched cords, coral stitch, and French knot. (Knotting was a popular diversion. Knots were spaced along a cord, which was then couched to embroidery or used for braidlike effects.) The appearance of these white embroideries with their handsome raised stitches is, in intent at least, similar to candlewicking.

In making candlewicking a long, large-eyed needle was threaded with several strands of wicking. A loop was made in the stitch, using a small stick or wire as a gauge. Then the loop was followed by several short running stitches. In early work the loops were not cut; later, both cut and uncut candlewicks were made. The appearance of the two types is quite different, since the uncut designs have greater clarity. Sometimes tufts were arranged in two levels, adding to the rich effect.

Early candlewicks were always white, but numerous variations in motifs evolved. Vines and clusters of grapes were popular, as were sprays and baskets of flowers. In the first quarter of the nineteenth century candlewick covers were made in designs similar to those used for trapunto work: flower baskets, berries, vines, pine trees, fleurs-de-lis, lettering, and numbers. There are coverlets made in geometric patterns, which often are the most distinguished in design. Some of the pieces worked by women are known to have been designed by men. Contemporary designers apparently are not exploring the possibilities of candlewicking.

Bedspread initialed T C and dated
1825 at one end and E S 1821 at
the other. Candlewick embroidery.
Metropolitan Museum of Art, gift of
Jane A. Everdell in memory of
Cornelia Augusta Chapman
Everdell, 1923.

146

Making running-stitch embroidery for cut pile.

Notes on technique

It is possible that embroidered pile rugs are indigenous to America, but other techniques practiced elsewhere are so similar that it is hard to believe that this simple one did not evolve in other places.

Pile embroidery is quickly worked and fascinating to do. The proper choice of foundation fabric and yarn for the pile is essential. The ground must be loosely woven but stable. A plain (tabby) weave with smooth warps and wefts of even weight is best. Wool usually was chosen, but linen also was used. If the ground is to be worked on a frame, the firmness of the material is less critical; stretching it onto the frame will stabilize it.

Exactly how the cloth was prepared for work in the eighteenth and nineteenth centuries is not known, but the size and weight of the bed rugs make it likely that frames like those used for quilting were needed. It is, however, quite possible to work without one. At the beginning, while the foundation is still limp and unmanageable, a small hand hoop can be used. As stitches are worked into the ground, it becomes somewhat stiff and bulky, and the hoop is no longer needed or usable. Although early pile embroiderers do not seem to have done so, it would be possible to make a large article by piecing together blocks or strips of embroidery. Seams could be worked over with pile, rendering joinings invisible.

The threads from which the pile is made produce a better-looking product if, like old hand-spun wool, they have some inherent wiriness and are not too soft. The rug should not mat down to a flat mass. In old rugs yarns with several plies were used, as a rule, but in a few examples two-ply yarns were chosen. The yarn was pulled through the ground fabric with a large needle. A loose weave and large needle make gauging loops easier.

Designs for pile fabrics must have large, simple shapes. Make some trials with the type of design and the thread that you intend to use. If you do not want to draw directly onto the ground fabric, draw the design in full (or half of the design, if it is to be symmetrical) on wrapping paper. If the ground is light colored, a transfer pencil can be used, but for either light or dark grounds a tracing wheel and tracing paper also are helpful. Whatever the transfer method used, the markings probably will require reinforcement if they are to last throughout the working period. Ink, if waterproof, can be used. On dark grounds white tempera paint works well. If the piece is to be laundered later, the white paint will wash out.

For a really large piece, make a photographic slide of the drawing. Pin or tape paper or the actual foundation material to a wall or other flat surface. Project the slide onto the cloth or paper in the scale wanted, and trace the image. This is one of the easiest transfer methods.

In making the sample shown here one-ply Swedish yarn of a homespun type was used. Three strands were doubled in the needle. Loops were cut as the work progressed. The completed embroidery is very pliable, more pliable than desirable if the rug were to be used on the floor, although the wool was worked very densely. (The stitches were placed more closely than on most bed rugs in order to get proper definition in the small-scale design.) Even so, the finished product is supple enough to be used for clothing.

If you hold the embroidery in your hand as you work, it will draw up slightly. If a specific dimension is needed, allow about a half inch additional per foot. For ease in handling, work should be started in the center. If the loops are to be cut, this should be done as work progresses. It is much more difficult to clip finished work. The easiest clipping is near an edge, so if work is clipped as it goes along, the cutting can always be worked from a nearby edge.

Motifs always should be started with two rows of stitching around the contour. Usually work will continue with concentric rows, working toward the center, but sometimes, especially in large areas, the rows may be in straight parallel lines.

As a rule of thumb, allow four full working days for each square foot of pile embroidery. The amount of time actually needed will vary according to the intricacy of the design, the spacing of the stitches, and other considerations. Whether or not the loops are cut will make a difference. But it can be estimated roughly that a rug consisting of 56 square feet of embroidery would require about two hundred and twenty-five days to complete.

Clipped loops look velvety; they have the rich luminous color of an Oriental rug, if good yarns have been used, although lesser yarns can be used to good effect too. Several colors threaded together in the needle make a fine mottled texture when loops are not cut. If they are clipped, the colors blend. Running-stitch pile embroidery can be expensive, because a great deal of material is required, but it also is a good way to use up odds and ends of yarn.

Cross section showing running stitch as used in bed rugs.

Cross section showing loops of a hooked rug. Two loops at the right have been clipped to make cut pile.

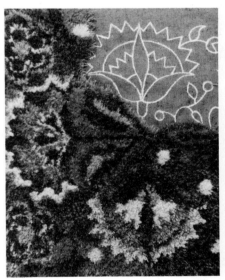

Work in progress on a cut-pile rug made in running stitch by author.

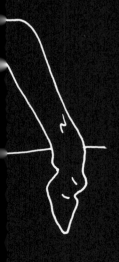

IV Surface Embroidery in Silk

Surface Embroidery in Silk

After the Revolution the vogue for woolen embroidery did not revive, for several reasons. By then, trading companies were bringing in exquisite examples of Oriental silk-on-silk embroideries, and these needleworks tempted imitation. The coveted cottons of India also prompted a new, lighter style in women's apparel, and while silk always is a preferred thread for needlework to be used on clothing, with lightweight cotton fabrics these fine threads become a necessity. During the eighteenth century furniture styles, as noted previously, moved toward the austere federal style. Brightly colored woolen embroidery, perfectly suited to a William and Mary room, would have seemed out of place in a formal federal setting. Last, but certainly not least, was the practical consideration that silk threads simply were becoming more available.

Among the Oriental goods being imported at this time (and throughout the eighteenth century) were large numbers of bed furnishings and bedcovers from China. These were embroidered in silk threads, usually in satin stitch, on grounds of various weaves. Painted and embroidered silk and gauze panels were imported as curtains and wall hangings. (Walls of English houses that lately had been hung with fine tapestry were redecorated with painted Chinese papers.) Silk or English broadcloth garments, cut but not assembled, were sent to China for embroidering.

Germain de Saint-Aubin, embroidery designer for King Louis XV, in *L'Art du Brodeur* (The Art of the Embroiderer, 1770), makes the point that Chinese embroidery was exact in technique, clean, and well finished. Much of it was worked on a vertical frame with a worker seated on each side. The needle was passed back and forth between them; finished work was reversible. The subjects most sought in the West were those understood equally by Westerner and Oriental: trees, flowers, birds, and animals.

In America, as in England, women continued to embroider bedcovers, clothing, pictures, and small articles. The scale of the motifs diminished. Whether the change from the monumental, deep-colored motifs of Flemish tapestry to the delicately tinted

Family record sampler made by Hannah Loring. Boston, 1812. Metropolitan Museum of Art, bequest of Mabel Herbert Harper, 1957. From the collection of Mrs. Lathrop Colgate Harper.

La France Rose, color plate of an embroidery design issued by Belding Bros. in the twentieth century.

Chrysanthemum. Belding Bros.

flowering branches of Chinese wallpaper was a result of the Chinese influence or simply a manifestation of the same impulse is a question that cannot be answered, but the elegantly conventionalized floral patterns of Persian bedcovers, also then being imported, certainly affected eighteenth-century embroidery. The use of a central medallion with corner quadrants and a powdering of small motifs reflects Persian composition.

Turkey work, canvas work, and surface embroidery in crewels looked appropriate with the heavy Jacobean furniture used in America until 1690, and even with the later William and Mary style which flourished for the next thirty or forty years. Cup-and-cover legs, bun (ball, onion) and paintbrush (Spanish) feet, and scrolled stretchers were bold forms. The great William and Mary innovation, the wing chair, was a fine background for woolen surface embroidery on fustian and for canvas work in cross, Florentine, and other stitches.

The breakaway from large-scale motifs began with the Queen Anne style, initiated in the colonies about 1720. This style and the Chippendale still were sufficiently robust to accommodate canvas work and wool embroidery. It remained for the federal style, the American version of English regency and French directoire, to oust woolen embroidery completely and replace it with satin- and chain-stitch embroidery in silk.

Before the federal style swept away the homely touches of former times, bright little silk samplers and intricately stitched satin-grounded pictures, similar to those made in England, decorated colonial rooms. Occasionally, an embroidered picture had a bit of relief work. The animals, birds, and flowers that appear on these pictures are identical to motifs in English pictures, and undoubtedly the grounds, like those for other types of embroidery, came from England with patterns already drawn on them.

The New England colonists were no less rank conscious than citizens of the Old World. At the top of the social ladder were the government leaders, clergy, the independently wealthy, the gentry, and the scholars. Next came merchants and landowners. At the bottom were the laborers, servants, and slaves, for although slavery was never as prevalent in New England as in the South, it was not finally abolished in the Northern colonies until 1804. Social distinctions were strictly maintained. Individuals were addressed according to their positions. In the meetinghouses they were seated according to their social rank. At Harvard, where not all the students were wealthy, class differences were recognized. People wore elegant clothing, if they could afford it, and to some extent, they

Hatchment of the arms of Isaiah Thomas. Silk embroidery. Boston, eighteenth century. Metropolitan Museum of Art, Rogers Fund, 1936.

used coats of arms. (Thomas Jefferson noted that a coat of arms could be purchased as cheaply as any other coat.)

Embroidered coats of arms are unusual among American needleworks because they are very formal designs worked quite precisely. Some were thread-counted exclusively. Others were a combination of thread-counting and satin stitch. Still others were worked entirely in surface stitching. Silk is the usual thread.

Crests were most evident at funerals, during which they appeared in hatchments placed on the coffin or borne with the hearse, along with banners and flags. The custom seems to have been limited to New England and was at its height in the mid-eighteenth century.

Apparently, however, the hatchments used at funerals usually were not embroidered. More often the crest was painted on wood or on a lozenge-shaped, stretched canvas set against a square background painted black. For married couples, the hatchment showed the arms of the husband's family on the left half and those of the wife's family on the right, with only the half that represented the family of the deceased painted on a black ground.

The custom may have originated in the Netherlands, where, in the seventeenth century, a widow had a hatchment fixed to her door for a year following the death of her husband, the period during which she was allowed to keep her house. In England and Scotland, well into the nineteenth century, a hatchment was affixed over the entrance to the home and then sometimes moved to the church walls, to remain as a memorial.

Men's Clothing

Silk surface stitching long has played an important part in costume decoration. Until the end of the eighteenth century men were still the peacocks, surpassing women in the brilliance of their plumage, although by the end of the seventeenth century men's daytime clothing already had become considerably simplified. By that time men were wearing the forerunner of their modern gear: coat, waistcoat, and breeches, although dress garments were still very highly ornamental. Coat sleeves were turned back to reveal embroidered cuffs and lace ruffles. The falling collar was replaced by a lace-trimmed muslin or linen cravat. Both men and women wore elaborately embroidered caps indoors. Both men's and women's gloves of the seventeenth century were elegantly embroidered and trimmed with lace.

By the eighteenth century the components of a man's attire frequently were made of matching cloth. Dress clothes were silk

Man's cap. Silk embroidery on linen. Probably Boston, 1725–75. Museum of Fine Arts, Boston, gift of Mary Whiton Hutchinson.

with lace and silk embroidery. The coat was collarless, fitted, had a full skirt with side vents, and pockets with ornamental flaps. Silk-covered buttons (with embroidery designed to match that on the border around the pockets of the coat) were placed on the front closing, at the top of the hip vents, and around the cuffs, but they seem to have been purely ornamental. Buttonholes seldom were opened. Waistcoats, equally decorative, were sleeved until mid-century, sometimes double breasted, but otherwise cut in the same way as the coat, except that they had no side vents.

Tricorns were carried, but seldom worn, because wigs were the fashion. Since men who wore wigs sometimes shaved their heads, a cap was frequently put on when the wig was taken off. A uniquely shaped one is shown here.

Fashion-conscious young men who had traveled in Italy were called macaronis (explaining the reference in the song "Yankee Doodle"). About 1777 pockets in the lining of the coat were introduced. The cravat was revived, but the neck-immobilizing stock was being worn by 1785. This consisted of several circuits of muslin wound around a stiff collar and knotted in the front.

With the exception of neckwear and the waistcoat, men's clothing had become much less ornamental by the end of the century. In the nineteenth century only the vest remained a subject for embroidery.

Women's Clothing

Although women could be arrested for wearing silk hoods and scarves in public in Puritan Massachusetts, the fact that there was such a law simply emphasizes the universal weakness for pretty clothes.

During the second half of the seventeenth century women were wearing a style called an open robe. These dresses were full skirted, with the front open to reveal a quilted or embroidered underskirt. At that time the term undergarment was used for petticoats and other items of clothing intended to be seen, but worn beneath the uppermost garment. A petticoat was a *petit* coat, worn for warmth, although it might be elaborately embroidered, quilted, trimmed in gold or linen lace, beaded, or fringed. Petticoats were made in all sorts of fabrics: taffeta, moiré, and other silks, linen, mohair, holland, and calico.

Necklines varied, but almost always involved lace or embroidery. Capes, shawls, and tippets covered the shoulders.

In the eighteenth century the open robe remained in fashion, but closed robes (one-piece gowns) were in style also. Separates appeared, the bodices and jackets shaped to fit over the skirt. Low necklines and short sleeves were usual. Bustles were in fashion early in the century and again at the end. In the intervening period various kinds of hoops were worn: dome-shaped, pyramidal, and oblong.

The open robe generally was open above the waist as well as below. Lapel-like folds at the sides of the openings were called robings and usually were decorated. Some of the finest embroidery was made for the stomacher, which filled in the opening between waist and neckline. Low necklines on one-piece dresses were filled with modesty pieces or neckerchiefs made of silk, gauze, linen, or muslin. All these were possible subjects for embroidery or lace.

Until the middle of the century elbow-length sleeves had turned-back cuffs. Later, they were ruffled.

The silk-embroidered linen dress made by Abigail Wadsworth, aunt of the founder of the Wadsworth Atheneum, is an example of the style of the times and an indication of how such beautifully embroidered garments came into being. J. Herbert Callister writes that "according to family tradition Abigail rode to Boston by horseback (on a pillion) to acquire the material and patterns, probably drawn by a professional. (There are small areas on the inside where the pattern has been drawn but not worked.) There are several small horses . . . along with the floral forms and birds, presumably to celebrate her ride to Boston and back."

Fancy bibless aprons were an ornamental affectation that remained popular until the end of the century. Although a great many of the aprons were white, trimmed with white embroidery and lace, others were silk, embroidered with silk in rich shades. Many English and colonial American inventories list aprons. Seventeenth-century aprons were long, but by the end of the century they were becoming shorter and sometimes were made entirely of lace. Embroidery was worked with silk and metal threads. In Queen Anne's time the nobility, even the queen, wore aprons. (Mary Stuart, Queen of Scots, had a collection of more than a hundred.) They were a fashionable addition to wedding costumes. But Beau Nash banned them from the Pump Room at Bath.

An eighteenth-century innovation was the use of a drawstring at the waistline, a practical device for aprons that were laundered, and certainly an aid in the preservation of the fine embroidery, as such aprons could be stored flat.

By the nineteenth century the vogue for aprons was on the way out, although they continued as a part of mourning gear for a time. In the 1850s embroidered silk sewing aprons were popular,

Dress embroidered by Abigail Wadsworth (b. 1735). Connecticut, ca. 1760. Wadsworth Atheneum, lent by Mrs. Frederic J. Agate.

156

Detail of the dress made by Abigail
Wadsworth. Wadsworth Atheneum.

and later, at the turn of the century, long white aprons of sheer, washable fabrics were made. Mull, organdy, batiste, and·lawn were embroidered delicately in white with repeated patterns of the type familiar from Cashmere and Paisley shawls. (One of these appears in the chapter on "White Embroidery and Lace.")

Normally women covered their heads. In the first half of the eighteenth century they wore pinners—circular caps with frilled edges that were placed flat on the head. Sometimes these caps had two long streamers called lappets. Later, coifs were popular. These were heavier and often embroidered. Mob caps of frilled muslin or cambric were also in style. Until mid-century they were bonnet-shaped with side lappets or kissing strings. These little caps often were worn out of doors under tricorns or wide-brimmed straws.

Silk and woolen hosiery sometimes were decorated with embroidery. Silk stockings made a very striking effect when their shiny surface was enhanced with silk embroidery.

After 1760 a sack dress was introduced and later, the polonaise, an open robe with the back section of the skirt pulled into puffs, became fashionable. It was worn with a sheer neckerchief fluffed full in front.

The basic form of women's dresses remained the same until the late eighteenth century, which saw the introduction of high waists, long sleeves, and full but straight skirts in styles intended as replicas of classical garb. Often the dresses were made of white transparent material. Elegantly worked border embroidery and sometimes small motifs scattered over the cloth kept to the classical mode. Made with court trains for formal wear, these dresses continued in style into the nineteenth century. Hats, shoes, and cloaks were trimmed with elaborate needlework, most of it imported.

Bustles appeared about 1815. Gigot and leg-of-mutton sleeves made broad shoulder lines until 1836, after which the line sloped.

American women kept abreast of the latest fashions through various magazines. In 1842 *Godey's* "No. 1 Improved Fashion Plate" appeared. Earlier, *Godey's* had shown the most recent styles, but with this new series the magazine not only provided carefully detailed studies of the latest fashions, but engravings of fine quality.

During the whole of the nineteenth century lace, tucking, flounces, beads, tassels, and braids were used. During the 1840s tucking and lace flounces were stylish. Embroidered or lace-trimmed muslin chemisettes filled in the low necklines of gowns. Tuckers also were used. Half handkerchiefs were folded loosely around the neck. Decorative tippets of lawn, swansdown, and lace were worn. Redingotes and spencers offered edges to trim. Even greatcoats were embroidered. The elaborate trimmings of bonnets and hats included embroidery, lace, and quilling. Silk embroidered boots were worn in the evening. A typical slipper of the 1840s had chain-stitch embroidery in silk, steel beads, a satin bow, and a silver buckle.

Umbrellas and parasols came into use in America in the mid-eighteenth century and were sometimes highly decorated. By the mid-Victorian era they had become mourning symbols.

Despite the amount of decoration on gowns of the nineteenth century, the use of embroidery was on the decline. Quilling, ruffles, braids, and various other ornaments created intricate effects, but were much less expensive and time-consuming to make than embroidery. The sewing machine was introduced in mid-century. It is possible that the incredibly complicated patterns for women's clothing that evolved about that time were the result of exuberance over the new invention; the superfluity of ornamentation also very well may have been a result of its introduction. The decline of embroidery may have come about in part because of interest in the small decorative constructions, ruffled and pleated, that could be made on the sewing machine.

Fashionable attire of 1857.

School Projects

Among the examples of silk surface stitching of the eighteenth and nineteenth centuries is a large group of samplers, pictures, and maps made by young women as school projects. The work is particularly interesting because it is the only body of work made in America under formal, continuing group instruction. The scholars produced embroidered maps, genealogical tables, memorial pictures, scenes from contemporary and classical literature, and even a few landscapes and maritime scenes. It is not always possible to be sure whether the needleworks actually were made in school, but aside from those with documentation, a sufficient number show similarities of subject or technique to make it probable that they were produced under some common influence.

Today it is difficult to understand why embroidery should have been such an important part of a girl's education, but of course at the time few girls received any education at all. The dame school was the only opportunity most girls had. Boys studied Latin, Greek, and mathematics. Girls were taught to read the Bible. Everyone studied spelling and penmanship. For some girls the only text was the hornbook, a single page on a wooden paddle protected by a sheet of horn containing the alphabet and a Bible verse. Sometimes it is said that the sampler was a means of extending the lesson of

Picture made by Evelina Hull at Charlestown Academy. Ca. 1812. Metropolitan Museum of Art, gift of Mrs. Joshua Marsden Van Cott, 1939.

Mourning picture dedicated to Josiah Torrey. It is labeled: Cermenati & Monfrino, No. 2 State Street, Boston. The firm was at this address only in 1807. Collection of Mrs. Gregg Ring.

the hornbook. Some samplers do contain about the same material that is found in the hornbook. Others have religious or pious verses, reminding us that it was the preacher who introduced many youngsters to books.

Fortunate girls were sent to finishing schools. The courses offered varied widely, some listing not only curtsying, deportment, and table arrangement, but also reading, mathematics, and geography, as well as painting, music, and needlework. By the mid-eighteenth century newspapers were full of advertisements for girls' schools and a few began to call themselves academies. During the Revolution many of these schools ceased operation, but by the nineteenth century the female academy and the finishing school were firmly established institutions.

The task of compiling a list of the early schools that operated in this country was undertaken by the Massachusetts Society of the Colonial Dames, and published in 1921 in *American Samplers* by Ethel Stanwood Bolton and Eva Johnston Coe. One hundred and twenty-seven schools that operated in Maine, New Hampshire, Massachusetts, Rhode Island, Connecticut, New York, New Jersey, Pennsylvania, Delaware, Maryland, Virginia, North Carolina, Kentucky, Tennessee, and Ohio are listed. Mistress Mary Trufrey's school, which opened in the South End of Boston in 1706, is the earliest noted. The latest is Mrs. D. H. Maundel's Seminary, 101 South Fifth Street, Philadelphia, which opened in 1833.

One well-known school in Boston was operated by Mrs. Susannah Condy, wife of Jeremiah Condy, the first schoolteacher at the North Writing School (1719–31). (Their son was the Reverend Jeremiah Condy, who served for twenty-four years at the Baptist Meeting House.) In 1747 Mrs. Condy died, and her patterns were offered for sale. The following spring her sister-in-law, Mrs. Abigail Hiller, opened a school. In February 1748 Mrs. Hiller advertised in the *Boston Evening Post* an exotic group of techniques that would be taught at her new school: "Wax-work, Transparent and Filigree, Painting upon Glass, Japanning, Quill-work, Feather-work and Embroidering with Gold and Silver and several other sorts of work not here enumerated . . ."

Another well-known school was Mrs. Rowson's Academy. Susanna Rowson, born in England in 1762, was a noted authoress and actress, as well as teacher. She married William Rowson, a merchant and musician in the Royal Horse Guards, in 1786. By 1790 he was bankrupt. He formed an acting company, which in due course he brought to America. For a time Susanna wrote, acted, and danced with the troupe in Boston and elsewhere, but in 1797 she left the

Stipple engraving, *Cymbeline*, by
Thomas Burke after a painting by
William Hamilton. Published in
London by John and Josiah Boydell
in 1795. Collection of Richard and
Jane Nylander. Photograph by
Donald F. Eaton courtesy Old
Sturbridge Village. See Plate 6.

Mourning picture dedicated to
George Washington. The glass mat
is inscribed: "Executed by Debby
Bates Sept. 1800." A related
composition, not a memorial to
Washington, is at the Concord
Antiquarian Society. Collection of
Mrs. Gregg Ring.

Mourning picture dedicated to
Alexander Hamilton. The
composition is based on an
engraving by J. Scoles, New York.
Another version, without the flag,
is at the Smithsonian Institution.
Collection of Mrs. Gregg Ring.

Mourning picture made by Mary Frost. The inscription is printed with type. Arlington, Massachusetts. Collection of Mrs. Gregg Ring.

This was the most prevalent of the early nineteenth-century Washington memorial compositions. Metropolitan Museum of Art, gift of Mrs. Russell Sage, 1909.

Another version of the Washington memorial picture, rendered almost entirely in silk-chenille embroidery. Collection of Mrs. Gregg Ring.

company and set up a school for young ladies in a house in Winter Street near the Mall, offering courses in reading, writing, mathematics, and geography, as well as needlework. One of her advertisements (quoted in Jane Giffen [Nylander], "Susanna Rowson and Her Academy," *Antiques*, September 1970), pledged that she would "endeavor by an unremitting attention to the health, morals, and improvement of her Pupils, to merit the patronage she now presumes to solicit." Mrs. Rowson's students included Ann Trask, of Gloucester, born in 1795, and two of her sisters (according to Jane Giffen [Nylander] in an article in *Antiques* in April 1976).

Ann Trask's *Cymbeline*, shown in Plate 6, provides an interesting example of the way in which students borrowed from other forms of art for their themes. The composition was derived from a stipple engraving by Thomas Burke, which in turn was taken from a painting by William Hamilton.

The needlework products of Mrs. Rowson's Academy and of other schools like hers were quite expert technically, but there is a certain conformity about them that makes one wish that the girls had been more adventurous designers. And despite a certain amount of expertise, few were equal to the demands that the growing interest in classical art put upon them.

For classicism was taking hold. The ruins of Herculaneum had been discovered in 1738, and digging there and at Pompeii had started the trend. On November 18, 1774, *The South Carolina and American General Gazette* ran an advertisement for John and Hamilton Stevenson, limners, in whose drawing and painting academy were taught, the advertisement stated, "Principles and Practice . . . after the Manner they are taught in the Roman Schools." They also offered to teach painting on silk and satin, "Designs of every kind executed in Hair; and in Hair and Colours, a manner never before attempted: Also Sewing with Hair upon Silk." The Stevensons' advertisement is typical in stressing a number of exotic techniques, but the straightforward offering of drawing and painting in classical terms is less usual.

The reason for the popularity of the painted-silk-with-embroidery technique is discovered in an advertisement in the May 23, 1797, issue of the *Pennsylvania Packet*, in which a M. Duvivier offered to teach silk painting that "may be executed with as much elegance, and considerable less trouble and expence than embroidery." Those who were willing to go to a little "trouble and expence" worked the simpler parts of their designs in embroidery and painted (or had painted for them) those parts that would have been more difficult to stitch (faces, hands, skies, for example).

Mourning picture made by Sally Austin at Miss Saunders's and Miss Beach's Academy, Dorchester, Massachusetts. Collection of Mrs. Gregg Ring.

Mourning picture made by Ann Vose. 1807. Bayou Bend Collection, Museum of Fine Arts, Houston.

Tulip, color plate of an embroidery design issued by Belding Bros.

Most instructors seem to have been interested in teaching techniques that called for patience and manual dexterity. Some academies offered courses in drawing and painting, but usually embroidery seems to have been worked according to purchased patterns or on predrawn grounds. Teachers, as well as professional designers, probably made adaptations (with varying degrees of skill) from engravings or other sources. Only occasionally does a work appear with documentation to the effect that the design was the work of the embroiderer.

The themes of samplers and pictures became progressively more somber. From stern moral lessons they moved on to mourning and memorial themes. This type of work was especially prevalent among the Moravians, who produced outstanding silk embroidery, had a long history of interest in silk, and had cultivated silkworms in Georgia. The Moravians founded schools for both boys and girls at their settlement in what is now Bethlehem, Pennsylvania. (The boys' school was a forerunner of Lehigh University.) The girls'

Mourning picture made by Jane M. Hewlett, Long Island, New York. A companion embroidery by her sister is in Stony Brook, and several closely related embroideries exist. Collection of Mrs. Gregg Ring.

Silk embroidery picture. Ca. 1805. Philadelphia Museum of Art, bequest of George L. Harrison.

school was presided over by the Sisters of Bethlehem, who brought the art of silk embroidery to a high level. In time branches of the school were established in other parts of the country, and this did much to spread the art of silk embroidery.

Memorial samplers worked in silk threads on silk grounds seem to have originated at the Moravian schools. The death of George Washington, in 1799, set off a period of mourning that was commemorated with many embroidered pictures. This theme called for formal treatment. The humans shown in the compositions wear classic garb and hairstyles. The monuments have a Greek or Roman cast. The gardens in which they are set are austere, with willows and cypresses, stylized and symbolic. There is an architectural feel about the embroideries and a cohesiveness of composition, as a rule. Some of them demonstrate a real effort to show natural depth and a specific scene in proper perspective.

Sometimes memorial pictures were embroidered with the hair of the deceased loved one in whose memory the picture was made. Often this hair was used to embroider inscriptions, which, because of the fineness of the hair, could be quite delicate. Fine line and pale silkiness are characteristics of the work. Sentiment abounds.

Usually, but not always, at least part of the composition was taken from an engraved model. There is always a tension between what the young needlewoman was able to convey and the quality of the original artwork, which the spectator can feel, if not see.

The grounds were silk in satin or other weave. Most of the embroidery was worked in silk, in satin stitch, long and short stitch, or

Londonderry, Ireland, painted in watercolors on satin-woven silk with ships and foreground waves embroidered in silk. Late eighteenth–early nineteenth century. Metropolitan Museum of Art, gift of Jennie T. Draper, 1922.

chain stitch. Heads, hands, and feet, as well as the vast expanse of sky, either were painted directly on the ground or painted separately and appliquéd to the composition. Chenille was used for trees and other subjects requiring heavy textures. It frequently is seen in later work as moss roses. Chenille thread was silk, about ⅛ inch wide, and had cut pile. Besides silk grounds, it was worked on gauze and open-mesh canvas. It remained popular until 1830.

Some silk pictures were worked entirely in hair. The tiny stitches, carefully worked into satin or other silk grounds, gave the appearance of hatching or stippling with a fine pen and ink. Landscapes and coats of arms were the usual subject matter.

C. M. McGown's view of "New York from Long Island" was copied from an engraving by W. Rollinson after a drawing by John Wood, published by J. Wood & W. Rollinson, New York, February 14, 1801. Its present owner, Mrs. Gregg Ring, of Houston, Texas, notes that there is a related embroidery in color (backed with an Elizabethtown, New Jersey, newspaper) at the Henry Francis du Pont Winterthur Museum. C. M. McGown was twelve years old in 1806 when this astonishing piece was made. Its embroidery is hair-fine black silk rendered in duplication of the engraving. The embroidery was worked over a print on silk cut around the shapes of scenic details. A linen ground is exposed only in the open area of the sky. The glass mat bears the legend "Mrs. Lockwood's Boarding School."

"New York from Long Island,"
made by C. M. McGown, 1806.
Collection of Mrs. Gregg Ring.

Design for a needlework picture
inspired by the monumental figures
popular with late eighteenth-
century painters and embroiderers.

166

"Malvina," by Mary Bacon, October 15, 1808. Silk and gold embroidery on satin-woven silk. Woodbury, Connecticut. Litchfield Historical Society.

A view of Mount Vernon was another favorite subject; several examples exist. They are unusual because the center of interest, the house, is placed in the far distance, an uncommon kind of composition in embroidery at this time.

Among the many embroideries based upon popular subjects there were some that succeeded superbly in their own right. The brilliant memorial to George Washington in Plate 7, possibly derived from an Enoch Gridley engraving, or directly from the painting by John Coles, Jr., on which the engraving is thought to have been based, is one of these. It is a tour de force of silk embroidery, rendered with all the glistening possibilities of the thread displayed at full intensity—with no loss to form or subject matter.

Among the languid mourning ladies of the memorial pictures, one of the most skillfully drawn was the large figure "Wrot By Miss ANN VOSE 1807," as the inscription of the glass mat states. The picture, possibly originating in the same school as the Washington memorial composition, is a memorial to Ann's mother, who died in 1807. According to Betty Ring in *American Schoolgirl Embroideries at Bayou Bend*, Ann's father was a Boston cabinetmaker and one of his delicate painted tables is in the museum at Winterthur.

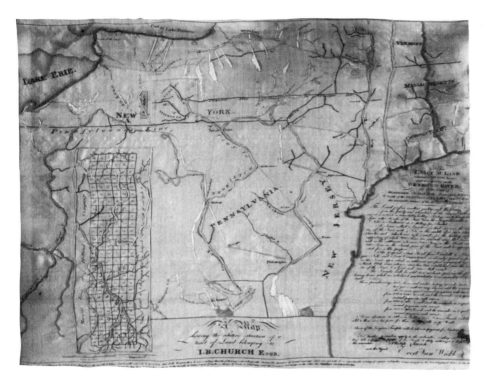

Map of Genesee County. Silk embroidery over copperplate engraving on silk. Metropolitan Museum of Art, bequest of Mabel Herbert Harper, 1957. From the collection of Mrs. Lathrop Colgate Harper.

Few schoolgirl embroideries are identified with the South. An unusual exception is an initialed and dated picture from Natchez, made in 1811, according to the identification embroidered onto it. In a letter to the author, Mrs. Ring, from whose remarkable collection of schoolgirl embroideries this piece comes, writes that much of the embroidery, including the French knots of the foreground garden, has been painted over, rather than embroidered in various colors. She suggests that a wide range of silk thread may not have been available in Natchez at the time, although she thinks that would be surprising, because by then Natchez was an old town.

A great many map samplers were made in England in the last two decades of the eighteenth century. These were seldom made in this country, although a number of handsome examples are known. Commonly called samplers because they are signed and dated, they have little else that is similar to other samplers, except possibly an enframing border. Some American pieces, like many of the English examples, were worked over engravings on silk. The drawings of other maps obviously were the work of the schoolgirls or their teachers. Map embroidery seems to have been an adjunct to the study of geography. In addition to the flat maps, small silk globes also were made.

Illustrations from "An Embroidery Lesson on the Sweet Pea," by T. Sanzo in *Home Needlework Magazine,* July 1904.

Not all embroidered pictures can be tied to school studies. Biblical themes were common. The paintings of Angelica Kauffmann, which are gently feminine, were popular prototypes.

In 1900, at the time of the Boxer Rebellion in China, many silk panels and shawls found their way to the West. These articles—embroidered with flowers, birds, butterflies, and other subjects, treated in naturalistic or conventionalized fashion—renewed interest in flat silk embroidery. Some of the needleworks were rendered in lustrous floss, some in duller plied silk, some in a combination of the two; but almost all the embroidery was very flat, worked in satin, chain, couching, and seed stitches.

Notes on technique

In September 1843 a "coloured rose and butterfly" was published by *Godey's Lady's Book.* The same rose, uncolored, had appeared in the July issue. A rival magazine had published a similar untinted rose in August. When *Godey's* colored rose appeared the next month, with it was published the following:

> We now give the real thing, and whether it cost little or much, we pronounce it far superior to any effort of the kind either in this or any other country. It plainly shows what can be done by an old established house, and must certainly, in future, prevent any attempts to compete with us. We are proud to add that the drawing is by an American artist and the colouring by an American lady.

The flower was red with green foliage. The butterfly, less faithful to nature, was brown and blue. The engraving was "Drawn by A. C. Smith" and printed by P. S. Duval, Philadelphia. This rose was the prototype of many that were rendered in needlework in silk and chenille, and it was, indeed, a very admirable addition to *Godey's.*

By the mid-nineteenth century women were released from the necessity of joining a class in order to obtain patterns and instructions. Both could be had through periodicals. *Godey's Lady's Book, Peterson's Magazine, Harper's Bazar,* and other later needlecraft magazines offered, among hundreds of mediocre designs, some excellent ones.

Many ground materials were used. Satin-woven silk in a creamy shade was most common for pictures, but a mixture of linen and wool or all linen also made an acceptable ground. Cotton was used less, although gauze and other lightweight cottons made pretty

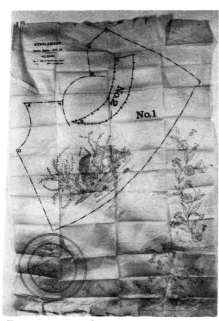

Pattern tissue from *Peterson's Magazine,* March 1884. The page includes a pattern for a pelerine with "Design in outline embroidery," a "Corner for table-cover; pattern in ragged robins," and "Design for painting plate or in embroidery."

grounds for silk embroidery. Fine garments were cut from damask weaves, ciselé velvet, rep, and other silks, which were then embroidered.

For silk surface embroidery the same stitches that are used for embroidery with wool can be used: satin, chain, long and short, stem, French knot, split, flat, fishbone, basket, varieties of feather, and couching stitches.

Both floss and plied silks are found. There is frequent mention of an Oriental crimped silk that appears to be only one ply of a thicker thread. Silk chenille was used a great deal. Metal threads appear to a limited extent. Human hair was used for fine black lines.

How to shade naturalistic subjects was a constant preoccupation of the magazines. An issue without instructions on this subject is an exception.

Diagram for embroidering a rose design in long and short stitch, from *Home Needlework Magazine*, July 1904.

Color plate of a rose and a rose design stamped on blue linen, from an embroidery kit offered by the Richardson Silk Company. The set included silk floss in green and shades of rose.

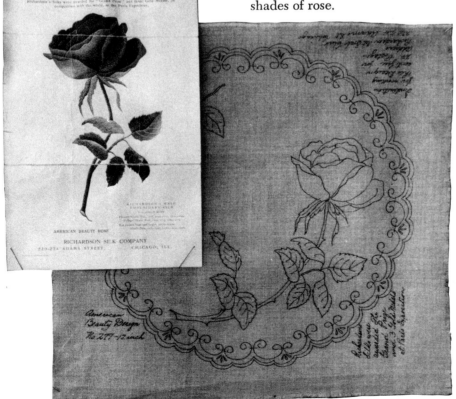

V Thread-Counted Embroidery

Runner, lambrequin, and table
cover. Berlin wool work, raised wool
work, and arrasene embroidery.
Nineteenth century. State Historical
Society of Wisconsin.

Thread-Counted Embroidery

Several techniques of thread-counted embroidery were very popular in the seventeenth century. It was worked solidly, as in tapestry-like needlework, and also in conventionalized border or spot patterns in various colors or all white, in black silk with metal threads or colored silks with metal threads. Embroideries of this type often were made to ornament the then fashionable undergarments that appear in portraits of the time. Blackwork was shown in some of the paintings of Hans Holbein, and the technique by which it was made now is known as Holbein stitch. Long samplers, or exemplars, made in England preserve a number of these thread-counted border designs.

Canvas-work pictures represented the most elaborate efforts of seventeenth-century needlewomen. These were extremely detailed, *horror vacui* compositions, with motifs dispersed evenly over the surface. Perspective and scale were not of great concern; detail and ornament were more important. Ambitious projects generally were not undertaken without assistance. Wealthy European households sometimes had their own designers and embroiderers. There were many opportunities to study embroidery, and numerous merchants sold patterns and materials. Skilled gentlewomen who needed to earn money opened schools of needlework, and there were professional embroiderers, both men and women, who took on students.

In America, Peter Pelham, who married the mother of John Copley, was a teacher of dancing, writing, reading, glass painting, and "all sortes of needlework."

Print sellers, including the painter John Smibert of Queen Street, Boston, offered engravings after Raphael, Michelangelo, Poussin, and others. Needleworkers had their choice of prints made from works by Italian, French, Dutch, and English masters. Such prints were popular bases for needlework composition.

In a March 1742 *Boston Evening Post* Mrs. Susannah Condy (see also page 181) offered "Pocket books, House-wives, Screens, Pictures, Chimney Pieces, Escritoires, etc. for Tent Stitch in a plainer Manner, and cheaper than those which come from London."

Hatchment of the family of Simpkins and Symmes. Boston, 1740–60. Henry Francis du Pont Winterthur Museum.

Le Soir (*Pastorale No. 12*), engraving by Claudine Bouzonnet after a painting by Jacques Stella. France, ca. 1667. Museum of Fine Arts, Boston, bequest of William P. Babcock.

Of course, only a few domestic embroiderers worked directly from prints. Many canvases, with designs based on such works, were, as Mrs. Condy's advertisement implies, imported. Professional designers made the adaptations.

Petit point designates work that contains more than sixteen squares per lineal inch. Before the eighteenth century some canvas work contained forty-five or more stitches per lineal inch. Needlework containing eight or fewer stitches per inch is sometimes called *gros point*. Several strands of thread may be plied together for work of this type. Actually, the term canvas is inexact. It may describe any of a number of types of fabric, but all of them were of tabby- or plain-weave construction. The fibers might be silk, cotton, or linen, but the warps and wefts were spaced so that cross stitches made over them would produce small squares, not rectangles. Such fabrics are called even weaves.

Flame stitch, tent stitch, cross stitch, and rococo stitch were the most popular stitches in the United States before the nineteenth century. French knot, bullion stitch, and other stitches employed in surface embroidery occasionally were added for ornamentation. The threads most commonly used were woolen.

Today needlepoint is the general term for all varieties of counted-thread embroidery that entirely cover the ground. In old inventories this kind of work is called "canvis work," never needlepoint. In the seventeenth and eighteenth centuries the term was reserved for an entirely different craft; needlepoint meant single-thread lace, lace made with a needle. (The other major category of lace, bobbin or pillow lace, was made by interweaving a number of threads.) Although the making of needlepoint lace has revived to some extent in recent years, it languished for so long that the original meaning of the term was almost forgotten.

Pocketbook in Irish stitch.
Probably Delaware, dated 1753.
Henry Francis du Pont Winterthur
Museum.

Pocketbook made by Mary Alsop
(b. ca. 1740) in rococo stitch.
Middletown, Connecticut, dated
1774. Henry Francis du Pont
Winterthur Museum.

Canvas work was used for pictures, upholstery, bed curtains, and cushions. The earliest American work is identical to English work; a good bit of it probably was made in England. At the Concord Antiquarian Society there is an unusual picture made by Rebekah Wheeler, the daughter of one of the first settlers of Concord, in "Ye month May 1664." Esther and Ahasuerus are shown in the composition, made when Rebekah was nineteen. The narrative is contained in a horizontal center band. Across the top is a border of landscape and sky, across the bottom a band of familiar beasts, flowers, and fishes. There is no perspective. A flower is as big as a lion. Main characters are larger than secondary characters. There is no suggestion of a middle distance, but this is not a peculiarity ex-

Bench cover. Eighteenth century. Museum of Fine Arts, Boston, gift of Miss Elizabeth H. Clark in memory of Mary R. Crowninshield.

Maple and mahogany chair with its original flame-stitched upholstery. Massachusetts, ca. 1760. Bayou Bend Collection, Museum of Fine Arts, Houston.

clusive to schoolgirl embroidery. Few paintings of the early Renaissance were composed to show nearby landscape. Usually a wall or drapery shut off that part of the scene from view. Art students of a generation ago knew this phenomenon as the "Florentine jump."

In addition to its thread-counted tent-stitch embroidery, made in the same manner as most tapestrylike Stuart or Jacobean canvas work, Rebekah's picture has some relief effects. The bodies are slightly raised, and the crowns are beaded.

Pictures with raised embroidery, now called stump work, are few in America, where energy was more apt to be spent making utilitarian needleworks. Flame-stitched canvas was used to upholster chairs and even to make bed curtains. (There is a set in the Sheldon Hawks house at Historic Deerfield.) This repeated type of design was a favorite, whether flamelike or in patterns based on a stylized carnation or on ogees or lozenges. A bench cover at the Museum of Fine Arts, Boston, has one of the most intricate of the patterns of this type. As in some others, the repetition of the color pattern here is not obvious.

The term Bargello, by which such work now is widely known, is recent and derives from the name of the palace (now a museum) in Florence that houses fine examples. It usually was called Irish stitch in early America, and is also called Florentine stitch or Hungarian stitch. (Few works actually were made in true Hungarian stitch, a combination of vertical stitches passing over two, four, and two threads, producing small, mosaiclike units.)

The quality that recommends canvas work for upholstery is the sturdiness of its flat, tight surface. It wears well. In the collection of the Pilgrim Society of Plymouth, there is a fine canvas-work card-table top embroidered by Mercy Otis, who in 1754 became the wife of James Warren. Her husband was later to become one of the presidents of the Provincial Congress. The daughter of James Otis of Barnstable, Mercy was a political activist and a Jefferson supporter, and author of a history of the American Revolution.

The embroidery of the rectangular table top was rendered in tent stitch. The shading is schematic, rather Oriental, with a deep jade-green background and flowers in red, wine, and blue. The design, simplified in the drawing here, includes upturned playing cards and fish counters.

A similar table top thought to have been made about 1740 by the wife of Lieutenant Governor William Dummer of Massachusetts has the same random dispersal of playing cards and counters, but more formal layout. The background is dark brown and the embroidery is tent stitch.

Pattern adapted from the canvas-work card-table top probably made by the wife of Lieutenant Governor William Dummer. The embroidery is now in the Museum of Fine Arts, Boston.

Adaptation of the design in the Mercy Otis Warren table top in the collection of the Pilgrim Society of Plymouth, Massachusetts.

Queen Anne style wing chair covered in its original flame-stitched upholstery. New England, ca. 1725. Metropolitan Museum of Art, gift of Mrs. J. Insley Blair, 1950.

"Piper and Shepherdess." New England, mid-eighteenth century. Museum of Fine Arts, Boston, Special Textile Fund.

"The Reclining Shepherdess." New England, 1725–75. Museum of Fine Arts, Boston, M. and M. Karolik Collection.

The Oriental appearance of the flowers in both these embroideries is due to the shading. Each petal and leaf is shaded with three or four values. On light-colored flowers this modulation gives a delicate appearance. On darker flowers the three or four tints include one that is very light and one that is very dark; there is no subtle gradation of tone. The effect is exciting, contrasty, and not a bit naturalistic. There are three shading schemes:

1. If one side of the leaf is light, the other side is dark.

2. If both edges of the leaf are light, the center of the leaf is dark; any veins are light.

3. If both edges of the leaf are dark, the center of the leaf is light; any venation is dark.

Of particular interest is a large group of canvas-work pictures that seem to have originated in a Boston school. Most were worked in tent stitch or other thread-counted embroidery. Their common element is the similarity of the main figure groups.

Like most pastoral compositions of the eighteenth century, these pictures are composed of three sections: foreground hillocks and ponds with flowers, animals, and fish; middle ground with pairs of large figures; and upper landscape and sky filled with trees, buildings, and birds. A few of the works are large chimney pieces, horizontal compositions having three major figure groups. Three have identical frames. Smaller pictures usually have only one pair of figures.

The groupings are not only similar, but some have been traced to their sources. In 1923 Helen Bowen made a comparison of eight related pictures in an article that appeared in *Antiques* magazine. By 1941 Nancy Graves Cabot could report in the same magazine that fifty-eight examples, including samplers and crewel-embroidered, surface-stitched designs, had been located, nineteen of them still in the hands of the families in which they were made. Later, the figure rose to sixty-five. The largest of the pieces is 5 feet wide, the smallest 10 by 12 inches. "The Fishing Lady" and her swain and "the Reclining Shepherdess" are the stars in this cast of characters, but some almost equally familiar supporting players are even more intriguing, because they so closely identify with one or another of the figures in a seventeenth-century French engraving, *Le Soir*, the work of C. Stella (Claudine Bouzonnet) after a painting by Jacques Stella of Lyons, her uncle. This engraving inspired not only American, but also English and French, needleworks. Hunting figures, derived from a print by John Wootton, also can be found. They appear, for example, in the foreground of the chimney piece owned by the Museum of Fine Arts in Boston.

"The Reclining Shepherdess," made by Temperance Parker. Massachusetts, probably Boston or Barnstable, 1750–75. Henry Francis du Pont Winterthur Museum.

"The Fishing Lady," possibly by Eunice Bourne. Wool, silk, metal threads, and beads on linen canvas. New England, mid-eighteenth century. Museum of Fine Arts, Boston, Seth Kettell Sweetser Fund.

Probably the earliest of the group was made by Priscilla A. Allen in 1746. This composition shows two of the figures in the Bouzonnet engraving. The inscription reads: "Priscilla Allen Daughter to Mr. Benjamin Allen and Mrs. Elisbeth Allen Boston July the 20, 1746." Priscilla's home was in Falmouth, Maine, but it is believed that she made her embroidery at school in Boston. Other examples from the group also were made by young women whose homes were not in the Boston area, a fact that seems to bolster the idea that the pieces are schoolwork.

Most of these embroiderers came from Cape Cod. Sarah Warren (1730–97), whose picture is one of the loveliest of the group, came from Barnstable. Her picture is dated 1748. For more than two hundred years it hung over the mantle in her home in Kingston, where she went to live when she became the wife of her cousin, the Honorable William Sever. Sarah's picture was made on fine linen canvas with silk and woolen threads. The predominant colors are reds, blues, and browns. The Fishing Lady and her friend appear in the center of the composition; Corydon and Phillida gathering pears are on the right; and on the left the Spinning Lady, another familiar subject, is shown. Across the foreground, in small scale, is a stag hunt, also a common theme.

Mercy Otis Warren, the maker of the card-table top already

"The Fishing Lady," worked by
Sarah Warren in silk and wool on
linen. Probably Boston, dated 1748.
Henry Francis du Pont Winterthur
Museum.

described, was the wife of Sarah's brother, James, a political leader.
Also from Barnstable was Eunice Bourne, who is believed to have
been the maker of another excellent chimney piece. Its composition
is almost the same as that in Sarah's picture, having both the fishing
and the spinning ladies, but on the right is a strolling pair based on
the Bouzonnet engraving.

Another composition was made by Hannah Otis, Mercy's
younger sister. It shows Boston Common as it appeared in 1755–
60. The picture is a notable departure from its contemporaries in
being rendered in naturalistic perspective. It appears to be an original design, and Hannah is said to have been proud of the fact that
it was not worked over a prepared canvas.

However, most of the pictures in the Fishing Lady series evi-
dently were worked over prepared canvases. The source of the
canvases may have been Mrs. Susannah Condy, whose advertisement in the *Boston Evening Post* stated that materials could be obtained from her by anyone who wanted them; they were not restricted to students of her school. Among the items she offered were
patterns for chimney pieces to be worked in tent stitch.

While surface-embroidered pieces were not made frequently in
the South, canvas work occasionally was done. North and South,
most projects were simpler and more utilitarian than the embroi-

Picture made by Priscilla A. Allen
(1717–85). Boston, dated 1746.
Henry Francis du Pont Winterthur
Museum.

182

Chair seat made by Anne Woodbury. Boston, mid-eighteenth century. Museum of Fine Arts, Boston, gift of Mrs. Kennard Winsor.

deries of the Fishing Lady series: chair seats, fire screens, and wallets or pocketbooks.

Many of the chair seats were beautiful. Perhaps these were exceptional because they were the work of experienced needlewomen, not schoolgirls, or perhaps it was because a fine chair was recognized as deserving of carefully designed embroidery. Whatever the reason, a degree of sobriety, order, and appropriateness characterizes these projects. Among the simplest is a set of chair seats now in Mount Vernon in which a simple shell motif is worked in an uncomplicated color scheme. At the time the seats were made for Martha Washington's granddaughter, Eliza P. Custis, the pattern had long been popular.

Floral designs, some composed to fit a specific chair and some with random patterns, were especially fine. Carnations were beautifully rendered in shaded tent stitch. Pictorial subjects like that in the superb, designed-to-fit composition at Winterthur also were used.

Samplers

Although certain textiles of great antiquity sometimes are called samplers, the precedents for the samplers made in America were

Chair seat made by Sarah Tyler (1718–64). Boston, 1740. Metropolitan Museum of Art, gift of R. Thornton Wilson in memory of Florence Ellsworth Wilson, 1943.

set by sixteenth-century embroiderers in Italy, Germany, and of course, England. In literature there are many references to the all-prevailing preoccupation of women with needlework, none more tersely put than these lines from Shakespeare's *Titus Andronicus:*

Sorrow concealed, like an oven stopp'd,
Doth burn the heart to cinders where it is.
Fair Philomel—why, she but lost her tongue,
And in a tedious sampler sew'd her mind. . . .

During the Renaissance women of leisure occupied their days with needlework, usually the decoration of clothing or linens, which required borders, fillings, and spot patterns. The first pattern book was not published until 1523. Before that time and until pattern books were widely available, designs were recorded by embroidering a repeat or two on a strip of cloth kept for the purpose. It also is possible, of course, that there may have been professionals who completed and sold samplers. But in most cases the sampler was a sort of record book, periodically increased by examples over a long period of time. (The term stems from the Latin *exemplar* or the French *essemplaire.*) Samplers were treasured possessions, listed in

Thread-counted designs derived from the Loara Standish sampler (ca. 1640) in the collection of the Pilgrim Society of Plymouth. Versions of these familiar patterns are to be found in many samplers, some made as late as the nineteenth century.

inventories, passed along as part of one's estate, coveted by collectors, and taken along on voyages to strange lands.

Records concerning English samplers, from which most American samplers directly descend, seem to begin with the 1502 Privy Purse accounts of Queen Elizabeth of York in the Public Record Office, where an entry reads: "the Xth day of July to Thomas Fisshe in reward for bringing of conserve of cherys from London to Windsore . . . and for an elne of lynnyn cloth for a sampler for the Quene . . . viij d" (quoted by Margaret Jourdain in *English Secular Embroidery*).

That samplers were valued is documented by the often-cited will of Margaret Thomson of Freestone in Lincolnshire, who in 1546 left her "sawmpler with semes" to her niece, Alys Pynchebeck.

In the beginning samplers were intended to be a reference work for the embroiderer, useful in the same way, approximately, that preliminary sketches are useful to a painter. Some never were completed; they contain wide areas of unworked cloth.

Many contain borders of needle lace, as well as white and colored embroidered borders. The lace was made at one end, the colored patterns at the other, and the white designs, usually in counted satin stitch, made a graceful transition between the two. Some of the earliest samplers were entirely needle-made lace. Ruffs, gorgets, coifs, cauls, handkerchiefs, and all manner of household linens were edged with lace, so such a sampler would have been as useful as an embroidered one.

Most of the borders of the sixteenth and seventeenth centuries are stylized floral repeats, some with a greatly stylized vine that looks more like Renaissance strapwork than anything in nature working a strictly measured, geometric course between the blooms.

Strawberries, roses, tulips, and carnations were the favored flowers. Human figures and animals were rare, but when they did appear, they were as likely to be a part of the needle lace portion of

Pattern for shell motif. The design is similar to that in the set of chair seats made for Eliza P. Custis and now in Mount Vernon.

the panel as of the embroidered part. England was, at the time, developing a type of needle lace unlike anything on the Continent. Its subject matter was more closely related to domestic raised-work embroidery (stump work) than to European point laces.

Many early English samplers still exist. Usually they are from 6 to 12 inches wide and from 24 to 60 inches long. Many are a loom-width long and have selvages top and bottom. The earliest pieces are true samplers, unsigned and undated, haphazardly arranged, with fragmentary patterns expertly rendered by experienced workers. On the very early ones there is metal embroidery and padded work in addition to thread-counted stitches. Possibly the first use of a signature in a sampler appears in the one made by Anne Gower in 1610, shown on page 10. Embroidered with natural white thread in cross stitch, it also is the first known example of the use of eyelet lettering in a sampler. The remainder of the piece is lace, described in detail on page 303.

Another notable sampler of the early colonial period was made by Loara Standish, daughter of Myles Standish. She was born in 1623, and it is believed that she made this sampler sometime before her twentieth birthday. The design of the sampler is typically English, with conventionalized borders. The embroidery, in a variety of thread-counted stitches, was worked with colored silks. At the bottom is a verse, possibly the first used on a sampler. The work is now in the collection of the Pilgrim Society of Plymouth, Massachusetts.

In the second quarter of the seventeenth century samplers continued to be made in this long, narrow form, but often their arrangement was carefully planned, and they were signed and dated, which may indicate that they were made under instruction. There is no doubt that by this time samplers were no longer rolled up and put out of sight in a cupboard. During these years they became tours de force, obviously ends in themselves.

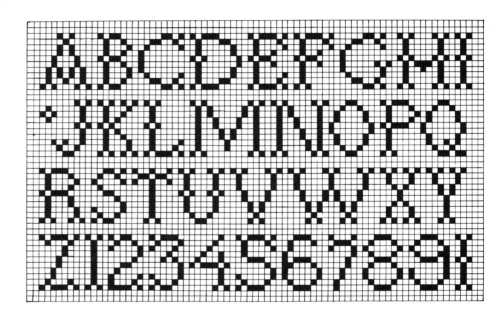

Alphabet in a style used for samplers.

The popular embroidery patterns of Johann Sibmacher of Nuremberg were published in England under the title *The Needles Excellency,* and by 1640 had appeared in twelve English editions. Sibmacher's designs for thread-counted work included conventionalized borders, running hounds, hares, birds, swans, peacocks, unicorns, heraldic lions, castles, and human figures in various costumes, including the garb of shepherds and shepherdesses.

In addition patterns were passed along by embroidery instructors (each of whom must have had a store of designs) or purchased already drawn in line on a piece of linen.

Seven seventeenth-century samplers in the United States, all virtually indistinguishable from English counterparts, bear remarkable resemblances to one another. They make it clear that in England at that time there was a strong traditionalism in decorative embroidery quite unlike the inventiveness that characterizes English embroidered pictures, although these, too, displayed common motifs.

The very long sampler format never really caught on in America, and by the mid-seventeenth century even English samplers were beginning to grow shorter. By the end of the seventeenth century sampler making was declining in America. There was no need for samplers; most women did not have time to embroider elaborate patterns in thread-counted stitches on sheets and petticoats. When the making of samplers was undertaken again, it was for a different purpose and in a different form.

Existing American samplers are of northeastern origin. Virginia was a more populous colony and certainly more in tune with luxury-loving England than life-denying Puritan Massachusetts. So why are there no samplers from Virginia? The answer may lie in the weather, or perhaps it had something to do with Puritan discipline. Probably the best guess is that a body of needlework was more likely to accumulate where embroidery was a school requirement, as noted earlier.

The long, narrow sampler of the seventeenth century was a dignified composition of tried-and-true patterns, an exercise in technical skill, not artistic innovation. It was, as a rule, entirely impersonal, but in many cases the care and patience of the mature embroiderer and her unprepossessing skill give character to these works that is lacking in most of the schoolgirl efforts that came later. They are, in short, some of the most attractive of all samplers, entirely devoid of sentimentality. Consider the verse of this one of 1648:

In prosperity friends are plenty
In adversity not one in twenty.

During the first half of the eighteenth century the format and composition of samplers changed. The long, narrow shape was dropped, and a picturelike rectangle took its place. The longer dimension could be either the height or the width. At first, the new shape was the only change. Samplers continued to have horizontal bands of conventionalized flowers and vines. In others much more lettering was used, and the bands became just barely recognizable as derivations of the old complex English border designs; they were scaled down, highly simplified, becoming, in the process, much more open.

In 1721 an eight-year-old named Mary Daintery made an 11-by-12-inch sampler with an enframing border. With the introduction of borders the transformation of the sampler from a study-reference object to a display piece was complete. At this point it is difficult to draw a line between samplers and pictures. Arbitrarily it is agreed that the amount of lettering is a factor in the decision, but not every embroidery that is signed and dated can be called a sampler. The point is rather irrelevant, because by this time both picture and sampler were intended as wall decorations.

Chair seat. Boston, 1745–65. Henry Francis du Pont Winterthur Museum.

Sampler making had become an activity of children and young girls. The average age of the sampler maker was thirteen, according to Bolton and Coe. Samplers were made not only by the daughters of families of means; some were worked by boys, some by slave children. There are samplers said to have been made by four- and five-year-olds. We are reminded that in the eighteenth century offspring were thought of not as playful children, but as small adults.

A trend toward smaller, more naturalistic motifs and gentler coloring was making its way in the decorative arts of the eighteenth century, as we have seen, and it is observable in samplers. It may not be easy to see a move toward naturalism in the stiff little scroll and flower patterns that were used as borders on many of the samplers, but in fact, they were. Precise, geometric strapwork was dropped in favor of narrow stems. Freehand vines, acorns, and strawberries replaced earlier, more complicated, conventionalized flowers.

Verses were fairly straightforward and objective. Mortality was a prevailing theme, though not the only one. Some typical verses:

This I did to let you see
What care my parents took of me. (1752)

———— worked this in great speed
And left it here for you to read. (1776)

Dear Child delay no time
But with all speed amend
The longer thou dost live
The nearer to thy end. (1713)

When I am dead and in my grave
And all my bones are rotten
When this you see, remember me
That I mant be forgotten. (1739)

Remember man thou art but dust
From Earth thou came to Earth thou must. (1756)

Time cuts them all
Both great and small. (1784)

Rug. Pennsylvania, early nineteenth century. Metropolitan Museum of Art, gift of Mrs. J. Insley Blair, 1942.

Sampler made by Susan Smith (b. 1783). Dated May 9, 1794. Henry Francis du Pont Winterthur Museum.

Death is a debt to nature due
that i must pay and so must you. (*1786*)

When I am dead and worms me eat
Here you shall see my name complete. (*1787*)

Of all the often-worked verses the most quoted are:

———— is my name
And with my needle I wrought the same.

———— is my name
America is my nation
———— is my dwelling place
And Christ is my salvation.

When this you see
Remember me.

Early in the eighteenth century samplers began to take on a distinctly American look. Little compositions with figures appeared, clearly the invention of the maker. Tent stitch and other thread-counted stitches continued to predominate, but surface stitches were not excluded. At mid-century almost every sampler had a border and contained a verse or an alphabet—or both. An arrangement, usually symmetrical, was plotted.

In England the traditional bands of the long sampler carried over into the shortened form. English designs became lighter, drawing became freer. In general English samplers are better in technique and are more disciplined than American work. They often look quaint, but seldom childish. American samplers, on the other hand, frequently appear to have been just a bit more of a project than the little person was able to cope with. The youngsters had splendid, ambitious ideas, but they often were a bit short on skills in drawing and composition.

Usually it is said that alphabets were embroidered in order to teach girls how to mark linens. Textiles were a valued part of a family's goods. All girls needed to know how to do plain sewing and to knit; fancy embroidery was not necessary, but desirable.

At a time when only four women in ten could write their names, it was considered learning enough if a girl could sew and read the New England primer. How ingrained this attitude was becomes clear when we read the verse that appeared in slightly vary-

Linen embroidery on homespun linen show towel. Pennsylvania Dutch, ca. 1800. Philadelphia Museum of Art, Titus C. Geesey Collection.

ing form on a number of samplers and is included as part of the inscription on the example made in 1739 by Margret Palfrey:

One did commend me to a wife both fair and young
Who had French, Spanish, and Italian tongue.
I thank'd him kindly and told him I loved none such
For I thought one tongue for a wife too much.
"What, love ye not the learned?" Yea, as my life
A learned scholar, but not a learned wife.

By mid-century, a base of hillocks and trees was being included in the composition of American samplers. This convention persisted in Pennsylvania, but elsewhere it developed into true landscape, sometimes very naturalistic, unlike anything in British samplers.

Architecture appeared frequently in the samplers of the 1760s. The large geometric mass that represents the building sometimes looks ungainly, but often is enlivened by some original and decorative treatment of brickwork, windows, stairs, or paths. Home, school, and important buildings in her town, or indeed, the whole town might appear in a girl's sampler.

The most accurate portrayals of the architecture of an American school were made at Saint Joseph's Academy near Emmitsburg,

Sampler made by Catharine Ann
Speel. Dated 1805. Philadelphia
Museum of Art, Whitman Sampler
Collection, given by Pet
Incorporated.

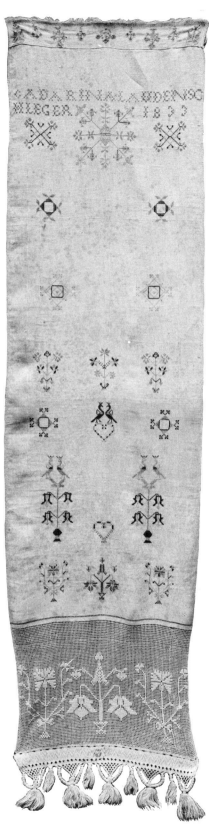

Maryland, which was established in 1809 (at first in Baltimore) by
Elizabeth Ann Seton, a widow who was to become her country's
first saint. The tall white building and other later structures appear
in numerous embroidered compositions, sometimes as the central
theme, sometimes in the background landscape. The pictures were
made not only at Saint Joseph's, but also by pupils in other schools
conducted by the Sisters of Charity, and continued to be worked
until the 1830s, according to Betty Ring in an article in *Antiques*,
March 1978.

In the third quarter of the eighteenth century rural vistas with
shepherds and shepherdesses, akin to the Fishing Lady pictures,
came into vogue. By this time thread-counted stitching often was
replaced in large areas of the work by satin stitches or other surface
embroidery.

Biblical themes, particularly Adam and Eve, were important
sampler subjects. An early Adam and Eve appeared in 1709, but
after 1760 many were made. At first fig-leafed, the pair was completely clothed by the late eighteenth century. The angel with a
flaming sword, frequently seen in Pennsylvania German fractur
painting, also appeared, but the Crucifixions, Lambs of God, and
churches that were favored by European embroiderers do not
often occur in American samplers.

Towel cover made by Caderina
Lahdenschleger. Filet work and
cross-stitch embroidery. 1833.
Metropolitan Museum of Art,
Rogers Fund, 1913.

194 Sampler made by Beulah Passmore. Dated 1813. Pattern darning on canvas. Collection of Mrs. Gregg Ring.

Sampler made by Patty Coggeshall (b. 1780). Bristol, Rhode Island, ca. 1795. Metropolitan Museum of Art, Rogers Fund, 1913.

Pennsylvania samplers were of several distinct types. One showed a building, sometimes a school, in a broad landscape band at the bottom. Name, date, and other lettering were placed in the center; side compartments were filled with geometric patterns, as was the upper band. A second type has a narrow border and a centered octagon within which are confronting doves and the inscription "An emblem of love." The same motif also is found in New Jersey samplers.

A type of sampler made only in Philadelphia was worked on dark-green linen canvas. Darning samplers, as well as more conventional types, were worked on the green canvas. Pennsylvania German samplers seldom have embroidered borders; a band of ribbon was sometimes used instead.

Among the many religious groups that settled in Pennsylvania were German-speaking Mennonites. They practiced the crafts of the Old World, embroidery included, and little from the outside world affected their arts. They took themes from the Bible or their hymnal. In addition to samplers, Mennonite girls included in their dower chests the so-called cover, or show, towels that would hang decoratively over the utilitarian towels in their homes. Cover towels were strewed with small embroidered motifs, almost always thread-counted, in color schemes of red and black or red and blue. There were initials or names and dates. Geometric figures, stylized birds, humans, and peacocks appeared on these towels in symmetrical ranks. The ever-present peacock was a symbol of well-being and good luck.

The eighteenth century, as we have seen, was a period of intense interest in botany. Baskets of flowers were enlarged and moved to the center in some samplers during the third quarter of the eighteenth century. Flowers continued to be a prime subject throughout the nineteenth century.

Occasionally maps were used in the composition of thread-counted samplers, though not as often as in surface-stitched ones. Like alphabet samplers, these were school projects. About 1814, at Westtown, a Quaker school near Philadelphia, the geographical theme inspired the making of stuffed, embroidered globes.

In the last quarter of the century genealogical samplers appeared. By this time, with the federal style in ascendance, surface stitches were used increasingly. Formal samplers with classical details such as urns, columns, and swags fit the style of the day.

By the end of the eighteenth century many different types of samplers were being made. Some were silk on silk. Others followed older forms and were silk on wool or linen. Hollie-point samplers with lace fillings on sheer grounds were another type; others, called Dresden samplers, contained various cutwork and needle-lace insertions, all in white. These samplers, and another type showing fancy darning, had no verses at all.

In the nineteenth century there was renewed interest in thread-counted samplers, usually worked in cross stitch. The motifs became quite static. Subject matter was little changed, but the execution was less careful. In England many designs were taken from pattern books and arranged into compositions. In the United States

Sampler made by Laura Hyde with the inscription (center): "Laura Hyde/her sampler/Æ/13 June 27 1800"; (left) "India within/the Ganges"; (right) "The outkast of the Kays Haram/the British Embas/sadors Lady ac/companied by a/ Grecian lady visets/ the Kays Lady at the Harem"; and (bottom) "Bay of Bengal." Connecticut, 1800. Metropolitan Museum of Art, Rogers Fund, 1944.

Sampler made by Sally Blunt, aged nine, includes the verse: "How blest the Maid whom circling years improve/Her God the object of her warmest love/Whose active years successive as they glide/The Book the Needle and the Pen divide." New Hampshire. Collection of Mrs. Gregg Ring.

there was less interest in book patterns, but compositions had the same general appearance, with small motifs rather widely scattered over the ground, often in symmetrical arrangements. Floral sprays, geometric designs, and lettered sentiments were the rule. Small figures frequently appeared, their faces worked out in a cross-stitched formula. Geometric borders and elaborate coiling line borders, which appeared in English and German samplers, were seldom used in America.

In Providence, Rhode Island, a number of exceptionally well-designed samplers, similar in composition and stitching, showed important public buildings. These samplers were completely embroidered, background as well as motifs, often with large areas of queen (now generally known as rococo) stitch. There seems no doubt that they were the products of students of the same school, probably that of Polly Balch. The buildings shown include the State House, Brown University, and the First Baptist Church, as well as the College of William and Mary in Williamsburg, Old Brick Row at Yale, Princeton, St. Ann's Church in Annapolis, City Hall in New York, Independence Hall, Carpenter's Hall, and various unnamed castles, courthouses, mansions, and main streets.

Two samplers embroidered in the manner associated with Miss Balch's school are shown in color in Plates 8 and 9. In Hannah Carlile's work, the entire linen ground is covered with silk embroidery in the major areas of the composition. The verse suggests that the sampler, although undedicated, may have been intended as a memorial. Research by Mrs. Gregg Ring, the owner, has established that Hannah was born in 1784, the daughter of Captain Thomas and Phebe Aborn Carlile, both of Pawtuxet. She was married to John Mathewson Eddy in the Congregational Church in Providence on October 7, 1804, and died in 1805. The sampler was made in 1796. The verse used (but with the lines broken to fit the composition) is:

Lillies blended with the Rose
Now no more adorn her face
Nor her Cheek with Blushes glow
Adding Charms to ev'ry grace.

Five years earlier Lucy Potter also completely covered the ground of her sampler (Plate 9), using both surface and thread-counted embroidery, including queen stitch.

Many of the samplers of the nineteenth century do not properly belong under a thread-count heading. Surface stitching became in-

Sampler made by Beulah Passmore.
Dated 1812. Courtesy Mrs. Gregg
Ring.

Sampler initialed A H and dated
1810. The cross-stitch corner motifs
are characteristic of the Westtown
School. Metropolitan Museum of
Art, Rogers Fund, 1913.

198 Sampler made by Hetty Rosalia Gruets. The eagle is a type often seen on Philadelphia samplers. Pennsylvania, New Jersey, or Maryland, 1820–30. Collection of Mrs. Gregg Ring.

Sampler made by Hannah M. Hillborn. Cross, rococo, tent, double running, stem, and satin stitches in silk on canvas. Pennsylvania (?), dated 1832. Philadelphia Museum of Art, Whitman Sampler Collection, given by Pet Incorporated.

creasingly important as the primary technique, and English raised-embroidery techniques were revived. Plush stitch was used for motifs in relief. Satin grounds encouraged the painting of difficult details like heads. The collage idea took hold; leather, chenille, mica, natural hair, ribbons, and quilling were added to embroidery.

Catchy anonymous verses were repeated on many samplers. Other verses were taken from the works of famous and popular writers. The Reverend Isaac Watts and Alexander Pope were quoted most frequently. Watts's *Divine Songs for Children* was used a great deal. A rhymed version of the Ten Commandments, on a sampler made in 1802, has been attributed to him:

1. *Thou shalt have no God but me,*
2. *Before no Idoll bow thy knee;*
3. *Take not the name of God in vain:*
4. *Nor dare the Sabbath to prophane*
5. *Give both thy parents honor due*
6. *Take heed that thou no murder do*
7. *Abstain from words and deeds unclean,*
8. *Nor steal, tho thou are poor, and mean*
9. *Nor make a wilful lie, nor love it*
10. *What is thy neighbours, dare not covet.*

It bears little resemblance, however, to the more graceful interpretation that appears in early printings of the *Divine Songs:*

Adore no GOD beside Me, to provoke mine Eyes;
With Rev'rence use my Name, nor turn my Words to Jest;
Observe my Sabbath well, nor dare profane my Rest;
Honour, and due Obedience to thy Parents give;
Nor spill the guiltless Blood, nor let the Guilty live:
Preserve thy body chaste, and flee th' unlawful Bed;
Nor steal thy Neighbour's Gold, his Garment, or his Bread;
Forbear to blast his Name with Falshood, nor Deceit;
Nor let thy Wishes loose upon his large Estate.

One of Alexander Pope's most-quoted lines was:

'Tis education forms the common mind;
Just as the twig is bent the tree's inclined.

Many samplers were very sober. Mourning themes, moral lessons, and registers of family births, marriages, and deaths account

Sampler made by Mary Ann Boyd in the same deep blue and purple seen in theorem painting on velvet. Pennsylvania, dated July 30, 1831. Collection of Mrs. Gregg Ring.

for a great proportion of the samplers. (The Revolution was seldom used as a subject.) Verses reflected the mood:

God counts the sorrows of his saints
Their groans affect his ears
He has a book for their complaints
A bottle for their tears. (1810)

No longer I follow a sound
No longer a dream I pursue
O happiness now to be found
Unattainable treasure Adieu. (1818)

Among the motifs not seen in the past were morning glories, lilacs, daffodils, violets. Flowers such as roses, which long had been popular, were given a new full-blown look, rendered more naturalistically. Other motifs were parrots and pets, stars, narrow borders, trees, single blossoms, sprays, baskets, vases, hens, doves, peacocks, roosters, dogs, lambs, lions, cats, crayfish, butterflies, keys, pipes, small boats, and houses.

Samplers were gayer and freer during the second half of the century. Many colors were combined; fortunately, most of the threads used in the samplers still were dyed with natural dyes and the effect is pleasant.

Notes on technique

In England many samplers were made on a fine, even-weave cream-colored cloth called tammy. Others were worked on pale-blue, green, or brown linen grounds. Bolting cloth (used to sieve, or bolt, flour) also made fine sampler foundations. In America linen grounds were prevalent. Most samplers were made on tabby-woven cloths, but there are a few that have grounds of other weaves.

In Dutch settlements and in seaport towns in Massachusetts a silk thread thought to be of Oriental origin was used for embroidery. It has a crinkled appearance that suggests that workers split the plies of this thread and used only one. Silk was the usual thread for samplers, but one also finds wool and linen, including a flat, shiny linen thread called flourishing.

Dyes were obtained from many sources. Cochineal, indigo, and logwood were imported; other dye materials, such as saffron, herbs, and *planta genesta* (broom, badge of the Plantagenets), could be found locally.

In the eighteenth century the predominant stitches were tent and cross; counted satin and line stitches were also much used. The plain cross stitch replaced the Italian cross and Montenegrin cross, two stitches used earlier in England. Late in the century satin stitch began to overtake cross stitch, and queen (or rococo) stitch was used a great deal.

The addition of large areas of surface stitching is the most dramatic departure in samplers of the eighteenth century. Couching, French knot, and stem, long and short, satin, split, back, rope, chain, and buttonhole stitches were used, among others. These surface stitches allowed greater freedom in composition than was possible with counted-thread work alone. The repeat-motif border was joined by a many-flowered type.

Darned samplers were especially intriguing. Squares were cut out of the sampler ground, then rewoven delicately in a variety of fancy weaves. Initially perhaps intended as exercises in practical darning, these samplers became works of art in themselves. The damasklike patterns worked into the darning probably never were used in actual mending. The samplers were, instead, showpieces.

In the nineteenth century, linen scrim, a meshlike fabric that made stitches easy to count, frequently was used for sampler grounds. Heavier even-weave linens continued to be used. For surface embroidery the ground cloth sometimes was silk. Darned samplers had woolen or linen grounds. Other samplers were made on tiffany, but this sheer silk fabric was fragile and brittle. A few samplers have muslin grounds.

Sometimes designs were drawn directly onto the ground with pencil or pen and ink. If the ground was relatively transparent, the drawing could be basted under it and the paper torn away after the embroidery had been made.

Oriental silk threads, the plies separated, continued to be used. Berlin wools were introduced, but they were too bulky for delicate work. Stitching was on the whole increasingly more careless as the years passed. The introduction of Berlin wool work turned many embroiderers away from sampler making, which had long since ceased to serve a practical purpose.

Berlin Wool Work

In 1840 the Countess of Wilton edited Elizabeth Stone's *The Art of Needle-Work;* in it she stated that in 1804 or 1805 a Berlin print maker named Philipson had published the first patterns for canvas work in which the designs were colored rather than coded. Basically, the patterns were copperplate prints, graphed and hand painted.

The commercial possibilities of the patterns were recognized by Madame Wittich, the wife of a Berlin merchant who sold books and prints. She was introduced to Philipson's invention in 1810. As an embroiderer, she probably realized that the patterns not only would provide a foolproof guide for needleworkers, but would be on the whole less expensive than individually hand-painted canvases, and her husband became the principal publisher of what later would be called in England Berlin designs.

Berlin Pattern 5760. State Historical Society of Wisconsin.

Philipson's patterns made visualization of the end result of one's embroidery a simple matter. Actually his patterns were the first to dictate closely how needlework was to be made. Earlier patterns were simply outlines that left matters like color, shading, and choice of stitch to the imagination of the worker. Coded patterns could not be too complex, or they became too difficult to read. Only expensive, individually painted canvas gave the same guidance as Berlin patterns.

The first Berlin designs were worked on tabby-woven linen or wool with silk or fine woolen threads, but in 1820 thick merino wools were introduced, and the basic stitch enlarged. The merino wool, made in Germany and used to work designs that originated in Berlin, came to be called Berlin wool, giving the craft the name by which it commonly is known.

Skilled artists soon began making designs for Berlin needlework. Works of famous painters were graphed for embroidery. Some of these patterns were very expensive. Designs from Wittich's original printing, patterns made from well-known paintings, cost as much as £40 each. By 1840, 14,000 designs for patterns for Berlin work had been published. Hundreds of women were employed in coloring the prints. Between 1835 and 1840 one publisher, Knechtel, issued 3,000 patterns.

Tinted and graphed patterns must have been known in England almost from the day they first were produced. Barbara Morris points out in *Victorian Embroidery* that printed textiles dated 1805 were made in England probably in imitation of these patterns. The designs were composed of small squares, each representing one embroidery stitch.

In 1831 a Mr. Wilks, who had a warehouse at 186 Regent Street, London, became aware of the Berlin patterns and imported a great number of them, along with materials to make the embroidery. These patterns and materials were sought eagerly by English needlewomen. Partially completed needleworks also were exported to England. In Frankfurt am Main an industry based on semifinished canvas work developed.

The mid-nineteenth century was ripe for a bold, high-colored embroidery. One of the trend-making events of the era was England's Great Exhibition of 1851. Flamboyance and inventiveness gave the exposition its special flavor. Visitors were introduced to classicized black and gilt furnishings, deep-hued wall colors, and upholstery fabrics in magenta, crimson, and ultramarine. The colors and motifs popularized at the fair found their way into Berlin work. Full-blown roses, lilies, primroses, and violets, naturalistically shaded and set against sharply contrasting backgrounds of deep red or black, are typical. The inspiration for these designs may have originated in exhibits like the complicated and colorful chintz sent by the French firm of Japuis & Son, with its incredibly large, detailed floral bouquets, or in a fine Brussels velvet carpet, which was a magnificent tangle of scrolls and palms.

By the 1840s Berlin wool work had made its way to the United States, and by the mid-fifties it was becoming popular. But during the 1880s it was already on the wane, although patterns were still appearing in some magazines.

Throughout its period of great popularity certain artists had deplored the undisciplined color and rambling pattern that characterize most wool work. In England, William Morris, Dante Gabriel Rossetti, and Sir Edward Burne-Jones called for greater attention to design. Lady Marian Alford deplored the low level to which needlework technique had fallen. In America, Candace Wheeler set about countering the deterioration by organizing the Decorative Art Society in New York. Later, along with Louis Tiffany and John La Farge, who were interested in seeing a strong crafts movement develop in America, she worked for the formation of Associated Artists.

Why all the fuss? What was it about Berlin work that was so upsetting? It made possible designs that were very complex but easy to follow. At first Berlin designs were made for shawls and collars, but soon ambitious projects were undertaken, sometimes by individuals, sometimes by groups. Often large carpets were made by a number of women, each of whom embroidered a block to be included in an assembled whole. Typically such carpets were floral, with a spot motif centered in each block. A 20-by-30-foot carpet, designed by J. W. Papworth, was displayed at the Great Exhibition. It was the combined effort of one hundred fifty women. Tapestry-like needlework pictures of great scale and complexity also tested the stamina of experienced stitchers.

Large embroidered upholstery pieces were sometimes made, but more often a less arduous project was chosen. Fire screens, chair seats, table covers, picture frames, footstools, ottomans, lambrequins, and cushions were made for homes. Note cases, portfolios, and carriage bags were decorated with Berlin wool work. Naturally, small items were made in the greatest numbers: tea cozies, napkin rings, bellpulls, slippers, pincushions, watch pockets, suspenders, match books or holders, shawl straps, tobacco pouches, paperweights, inkstands, key rings, shaving books, and the emblem of the day, the whatnot. Stiff Berlin wool work was not especially appropriate for garment decoration, but it was used to some extent for this purpose as well.

A tally of leading American women's magazines (made in connection with a study of the Helen Louise Allen collection of textiles at the University of Wisconsin under the direction of Otto Thieme) shows that the most-published designs were for borders, slippers, cushions, and chair seats, followed by footstool covers, traveling satchels, and lambrequins. A list of items for which patterns were published provides an insight into the extent to which Berlin wool work flourished in the United States.

For the home there were cushions, ottomans, chair seats and backs, game-table tops, footstools, bellpulls, rugs, ornamental brackets, lambrequins, light screens, reclining chairs, mats for lamps and trays, fire screens, cradle covers, window-seat covers, wastebaskets, cornices, bed foundations, curtain borders, door hangings, and napkin rings. Men used braces, boots, slippers, traveling satchels, gold-dollar purses, smoking caps, wallets, brush cases, cigar cases, ashtray covers, and key pockets done in wool work. For women there were purses, slippers, needlebooks, pocketbooks, workbags and work baskets, pincushions, hand screens, and foot muffs. Wool work also found its way onto borders, bookmarks, spectacle cases, cardcases, railway and carriage bags, carriage rugs, traveling blankets, and thermometer stands.

Mark Twain, in *Life on the Mississippi*, referred to a Berlin wool rendition of an engraving showing Washington crossing the Delaware as having been worked in "thunder-and-lightning crewels."

Oddly, the subject matter least appropriate for canvas work was the type most in favor. Work was admired for the intricacy of its detail and the complexity of its shading. Unfortunately, because of the coarseness of the technique, human and animal portraits, beloved by the makers of Berlin wool work, almost always became grotesque when translated into large, square stitches. This difficulty did not deter the designers of the graphed patterns. Numerous portraits of Washington and Franklin were made, none completely

205

Cover for table fire screen. Berlin wool work in silk and wool. 1860–80. Helen Louis Allen Textile Collection, University of Wisconsin.

satisfying. In England the rage for naturalistic portraits ebbed about 1840, to be replaced by a rage for equally naturalistic, usually overly sentimental Biblical scenes. Landscapes and historical episodes also were popular.

The adaptation of famous paintings to charted designs became an artistic specialty. Incredibly, some people thought the needleworks superior to the original paintings.

The awakening to the Middle Ages led by Rossetti and Burne-Jones and others resulted in the troubadour style of painting, a flattish, pseudo-medieval style. This resulted in some designs more appropriate for Berlin wool work, but for the great mass of embroiderers sentimental themes and naturalistic detail held more appeal. Embroiderers did not shrink from tragic themes or events of historical significance.

Sir Edwin Landseer's (1802–73) animal paintings, which were widely known through engravings made from them, were a favorite source of animal designs. Victorian passion for the overly domesticated animal is amply documented in Berlin wool work. In England the Prince of Wales in a tartan, with his pet dog, was a favorite composition. In America boy and dog were equally popular. The pampered pet, indolent on its cushion, was a subject of much canvas work. Parrots, also frequently seen, were derived from Edward Lear's *Illustrations of the Family of "Psittacidae" or Parrots* (1832).

Simple compositions showing animals, birds, or botanical themes were quite successful. They are without dramatic narrative and excessive sentimentality and do not display the discomfiting traits of much Berlin wool work.

Throughout the period of Berlin work floral designs were popular. In the 1830s and 1840s the flowers were depicted in normal scale against light backgrounds. Roses, poppies, dahlias, auriculas, and passion flowers were dominant. By mid-century the favorites were outsize, full-ripe roses, peonies, and lilies; a black or dark-hued background cast the blooms into sharp relief. Not content with dramatic shading, some embroiderers worked the flowers in startling three-dimensional renderings, using pile embroidery sheared in natural reliefs.

Geometric motifs, frets, and arabesques, perfectly suited to counted-thread work, were not neglected entirely; some of the most effective Berlin wool work contains areas of flat, highly conventionalized pattern. Lace designs adapt easily to the graph, and in the 1840s patterns in imitation of black lace appeared. To heighten their effectiveness, the background sometimes was embroidered in wool and the lace design in silk.

Then, in the 1860s and 1870s, while floral and other compositions continued to be worked, geometric and ornamental patterns became a fad.

The footstool cover shown in Plate 10 is from this late period. It is worked in tent and half cross stitches in salmon, beige, yellow, and pink silk, and wool in three shades of red-brown, blue-green, yellow-green, and red, and black that has faded to a dark green, on canvas that has twenty-six threads to the inch. Otto Thieme, who has photographed many of the items in the collection that includes this cover, notes that the Berlin wool work embroideries show a consistency in the number of shades of each color used. Stylized vines, acanthus scrolls, folded ribbons with schematic shading, Greek key borders, stepped designs, herringbones, and diapered repeats became popular. Flame designs, zigzags, basket weaves— many with shaded, overlapping arrangements—were used. Box and border patterns, lozenges, hexagons, octagons, and interlocking straps were perfectly suited to the large stitches of Berlin wool work. Alphabets and numerals, holdovers from the sampler era, continued in use. There also were small motifs from nature: oak leaves, shells, rosebuds, wreaths, floral sprays, small trees, small human figures, and others. Scrolls, harps, crowns, lyres, crosses (sometimes entwined with ivy), baskets, cornucopias, and anchors appeared. There were in addition the inevitable sentimental subjects: graves, urns, pets.

Small, neat motifs in restrained colors replaced naturalistic flowers, animals, and birds in magenta, purple, and viridian. Designs were taken from the pattern books of Adam, Chippendale, and Sheraton. The initial charm of aniline dyes was wearing off, and the influence of Art Needlework began to take hold.

Berlin Pattern 7409. State Historical Society of Wisconsin.

Notes on technique

At first the graphed designs of Berlin wool work were worked on plain-woven cloth, usually linen, with fine silk or woolen thread or on Berlin canvas, which was made of silk and was attractive, but not sturdy enough for heavy woolen needlework. It was available in many colors, the most popular being black, wine, and some whites, and could be purchased in widths ranging from an inch to a yard and a half wide and in four mesh sizes, having twenty-one, twenty-nine, thirty-four, or forty threads per inch. Silk canvas was quite transparent. Thread ends had to be carried back into embroidery of the same color, or they would show through. Berlin canvas was costly, very evenly woven, and appropriate for work in beads and chenille as well as silk.

Fold-out design for Berlin wool work from *Peterson's Magazine*, January 1888. Collection of Otto Thieme. Photograph by the author.

When thicker woolen threads were developed, about 1820, a more substantial ground became necessary, and a cotton canvas with spaced meshes was developed. An early cotton mesh, made before 1830, was not strong enough or stiff enough to be satisfactory, but for ease of counting each tenth thread was dyed. This canvas was not appropriate for embroidery with a white ground. The colored threads were apt to show through the stitching.

Cotton canvases were manufactured in England, Germany, and France, but the strongest and most evenly woven came from France. For needlework that was to have no background embroidery a German-made woolen canvas was available. Bolting cloth, an English product used for children's samplers, also could be used to work graphed patterns.

Penelope canvas, with its paired warps and wefts, was an innovation of the nineteenth century that helped to prevent stitches from pulling the ground out of shape. Earlier needleworks may appear to have been worked on penelope canvas, but inspection will invariably show that in such works the appearance of paired threads is the result of tightly worked stitching, and an unworked portion of the canvas will show a plain, tabby weave.

Mesh sizes were not standardized, but the most widely used canvases had ten to twenty threads per inch. The canvas was stretched in a frame, with the selvages along the braced sides. Work began either in the center or in the darkest part of the composition. Both procedures were efforts to keep the threads fresh as long as possible. Usually background embroidery began at the lower left.

Threads were not knotted, but worked back into completed parts of the needlework. (A needleworker today may choose, for convenience, to make a knot in the end of the thread, which then is inserted with the knot on the face of the embroidery a little distance ahead of the place where the work is to begin. Later, when the thread on the underside of the embroidery between the knot and the beginning of the stitching has been worked over with needlework, the knot can be clipped off.)

Among the more delicate products of the period were small tent-stitch pictures worked in silk on scrim. Some of the ground fabric was left free of embroidery and later backed with another, sturdier cloth. Satin-woven silks provided a soft sheen behind the scrim grounds of some of these needleworks.

In another variation of technique, stitching was done on canvas over cloth. When the embroidery was complete, the canvas was removed from behind the stitches by pulling it out, thread by thread, leaving the cloth ground. The background was not embroidered.

Another ground was a perforated cardboard prepared for use with woolen or silk thread.

Since complicated designs of the sort published by Wittich were expensive, a pattern might be resold to the print seller after the embroiderer had finished with it, then passed along to another buyer, presumably at a slightly reduced price. In this way designs were kept in circulation for a long time, making dating of the needleworks difficult.

Many Berlin patterns were vignettes. Such designs could be applied to numerous items. In America patterns began to appear in periodicals in 1856 and continued to be popular through the 1870s, but by the 1890s they had disappeared. *Godey's Lady's Book* and *Peterson's Magazine* began publishing Berlin patterns in the 1850s. *Harper's Bazar* was introduced in 1867 and immediately began to print patterns for Berlin wool work. Occasionally, *Godey's* and *Peterson's* published the same pattern. *Harper's* often duplicated the patterns in *Der Bazar,* a German publication. In 1870 *Peterson's* was publishing one colored pattern each month. The magazine was proud of the quality of its Berlin patterns and claimed that they would, individually, bring fifty cents apiece in a shop. As a seasonal offering, *Peterson's* printed a full-color, fold-out engraving each New Year. *Leslie's Ladies' Gazette* also published patterns.

The "Berlin wool" used to work the graphed patterns came from the fleece of merino sheep, a breed introduced to Saxony from Spain about 1765. The soft, silky fibers took dye easily and the threads made with them were brighter in color and had a finer sheen than other woolen thread. The Germans were excellent dyers. Wool dyed in Berlin was spun into yarn at Gotha and sold under the Zephyr label. Another, sturdier, worsted yarn, known by its Hamburg label, also was made in Germany. Like Berlin wool, it was dyed in a fine array of colors.

By 1830 merino threads had superseded crewels in American embroidery. Although merino sheep had been introduced to America early in the nineteenth century, the yarns produced were relatively slow in gaining favor, and for a long time much of the yarn was imported.

Berlin wool, or Zephyr merino, came in small skeins. The finest grade was called Split Zephyr. Two or three strands were needed when the canvas was fairly coarse. Sometimes English workers embroidered motifs in German wool, then filled in the background with English wool, which was stronger.

Silk threads also were used in Berlin wool work for grounding and accents. Floss silks gave a handsome sheen, but were not very

Embroidery designs issued as New Year's gifts by *Peterson's Magazine* in 1885 and 1886. Collection of Otto Thieme. Photograph by the author.

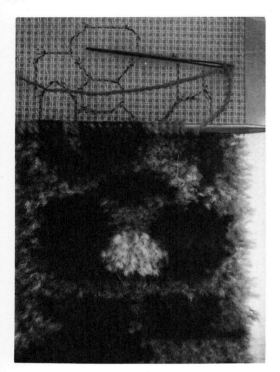

Working a design in plush stitch on double-mesh canvas.

strong. Another type of silk thread, mitorse, was half-twisted, and so a little sturdier. Filoselle, although not high-quality silk (it came from the outer fibers of the cocoon), was good looking and gave the work a pleasant glow. Metal passing threads also occasionally were used, sometimes for accents and, very rarely, for grounding. Chenille and beads might be used for raised effects in canvas work. Beads could be threaded into woolen or heavy silk stitches, or patterns could be done in such a way that fine working threads were not visible.

One of the differences between Berlin wool work and earlier canvas work was a difference of color. The first aniline dyes synthesized by William Henry Perkin (1838–1907) were purple or mauve. He developed them in 1856, while working on a substitute for quinine. He soon obtained patents, and by 1857, with his father's and brother's assistance, he was manufacturing the dyes at Greenford Green. Shortly afterward, alizarin crimson, a substitute for madder root reds, was produced.

Synthetic dyes seem to have been an instant success. To needlewomen accustomed to the long, tedious processes required to produce even soft shades, the strength and brilliance of aniline colors must have seemed miraculous. But for the unwary the potency of the new colors was a pitfall.

Before the invention of aniline dyes, yarns were colored with vegetable or mineral matter obtained from such sources as madder, indigo, quercitron, or manganese. The color range was dominated by browns, blues, and yellows. As new aniline colors became available, subject matter was shifted to show off the latest introduction. Thus, when alizarin was introduced to the market, needleworked gloxinias and fuchsias flourished. The fads for violets, lilacs, and tiger lilies coincide with the introduction of other dyes.

The muted shades used initially in Berlin wool work gave way to a palette of hard, strong colors, which, if not judiciously handled, could produce a jarring result. Even before the introduction of aniline dyes the number of hues and tints marketed commercially was remarkable. Each color came in a broad range of values, from almost white to almost black. Estimates of the number of shades available vary widely. According to the most extravagant figure, there were a thousand tints from which to choose. A more realistic-sounding count puts the number at about two hundred seventy-five.

In the 1850s and 1860s pastel shades were popular. In the 1870s Prussian blue was prominent, and by the late 1880s colors generally had become quite dark, with wines and maroons, olive green, brown, and gray favored hues.

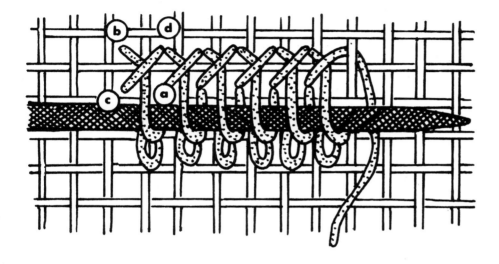

As the years progressed, stitches that were less time consuming were introduced. Leviathan stitch was one of these. Perspective stitch added a relief effect. The number of stitches proliferated, and in 1847 Mrs. Henry Owen's *The Illuminated Book of Needlework* was published, containing thirty-two canvas stitches. In this book the stitch that now is called Florentine or flame, and earlier was called Irish stitch, is listed as Berlin stitch. Sometimes in making these large stitches, which required more than one strand to cover the canvas adequately, threads of different shades were combined to produce a slightly mottled effect.

Tramé was another technique that assisted in covering when the stitch was large. A thread was laid across a row of meshes, then cross or tent stitch was worked over it.

Plush stitch produced high relief; the pile always was sheared to make intricately carved effects. The naturalistic look of a parrot, for example, was heightened by working it in plush stitch, then carving the pile to resemble the contours of the bird's body. Plush stitch also could be used for fur effects.

Embroidery with silk presented different problems, and when these shiny threads were used in Berlin work, it was thought best to control the gloss by working the silk in small, gemlike patterns.

The list of stitches used in Berlin wool work is a long one, but by far the greatest number of articles was worked in tent, cross, or Berlin (Florentine) stitch, which allowed the greatest intricacy in the design. These and other stitches used in various forms of thread-counted embroidery are shown here.

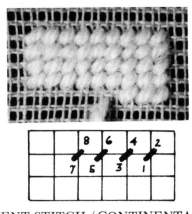

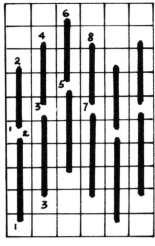

TENT STITCH (CONTINENTAL
STITCH, PETIT POINT).

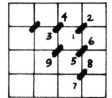

FLORENTINE STITCH (IRISH
STITCH, FLAME STITCH,
BARGELLO, BERLIN STITCH).

BASKET WEAVE (DIAGONAL
STITCH, BIAS TENT STITCH).

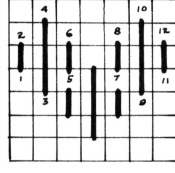

HUNGARIAN STITCH.

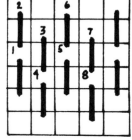

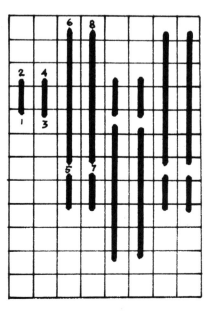

BRICK STITCH (ALTERNATING
STITCH).

OLD FLORENTINE STITCH.

212

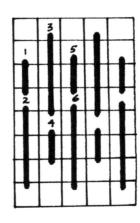

PARISIAN STITCH.

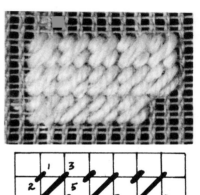
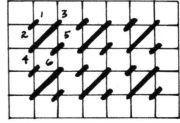

MOSAIC STITCH (HUNGARIAN MOSAIC STITCH).

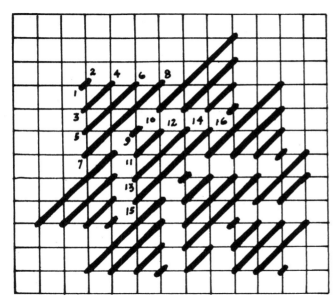

MILANESE STITCH.

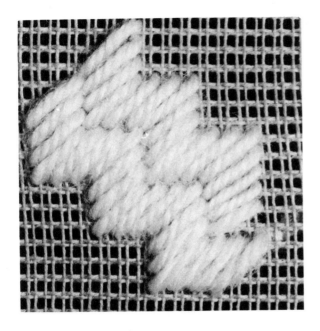
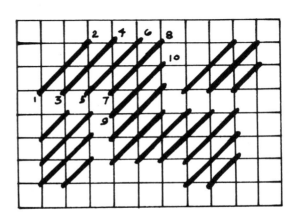

BYZANTINE STITCH.

214

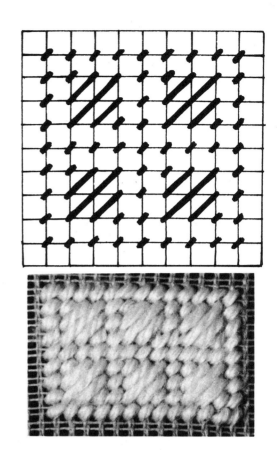

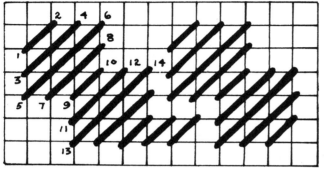

SCOTCH STITCH.

SCOTCH STITCH VARIATION.

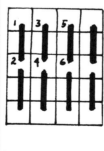

UPRIGHT GOBELIN
(STRAIGHT GOBELIN,
RENAISSANCE STITCH).

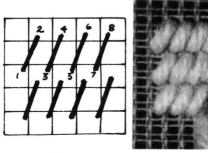

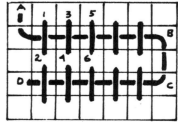

SLANTING GOBELIN
(OBLIQUE GOBELIN).

UPRIGHT GOBELIN WORKED
OVER TRAMÉ TO RAISE THE
STITCH.

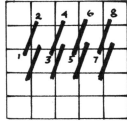

INTERLOCKING GOBELIN
(ENCROACHING GOBELIN).

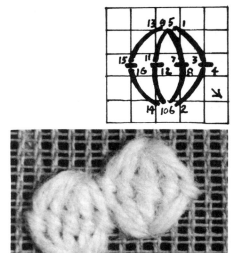

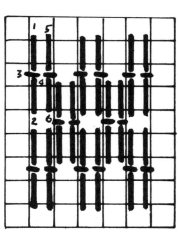

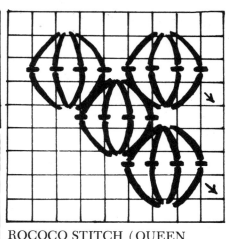

215

ROCOCO STITCH (QUEEN
STITCH).

PLAITED GOBELIN.

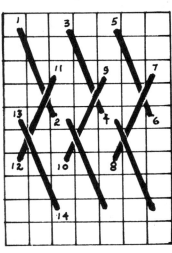

FRENCH STITCH.

ENCROACHING OBLIQUE
STITCH.

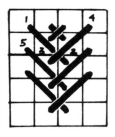

FERN STITCH.

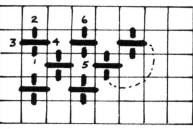

UPRIGHT CROSS STITCH.

216

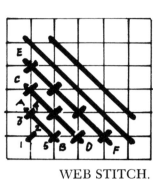
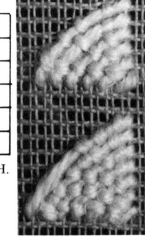

WEB STITCH.

OBLONG CROSS STITCH.

KNOTTED STITCH.

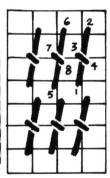

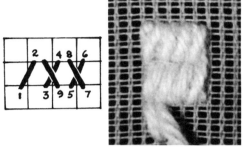

RICE STITCH (CROSSED
CORNERS CROSS STITCH).

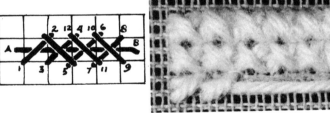

CROSS STITCH TRAMÉ.

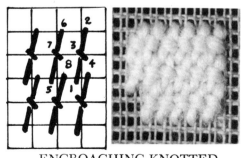

ENCROACHING KNOTTED
STITCH.

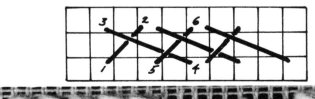

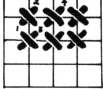

CROSS STITCH.

LONG-ARMED CROSS STITCH
(GREEK STITCH).

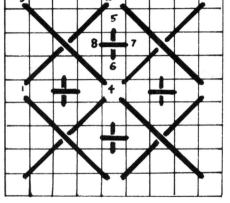

DOUBLE CROSS STITCH.

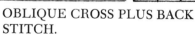

OBLIQUE CROSS PLUS BACK
STITCH.

217

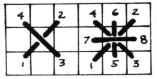

SMYRNA CROSS
STITCH.

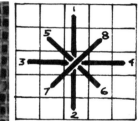

DOUBLE STITCH.

DOUBLE STRAIGHT CROSS STITCH.

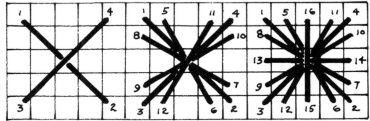

DOUBLE LEVIATHAN STITCH.

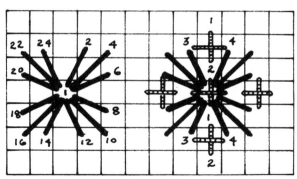

TRIPLE LEVIATHAN STITCH.

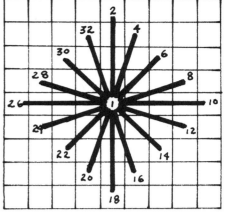

DIAMOND EYELET STITCH.

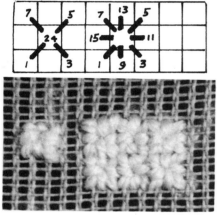

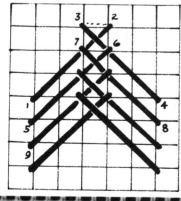

STAR STITCH (ALGERIAN EYE
STITCH).

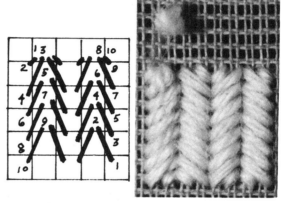

KALEM STITCH (REVERSE
TENT STITCH).

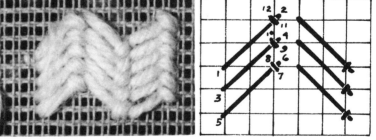

FISHBONE STITCH (LONG
AND SHORT STITCH).

VAN DYKE STITCH.

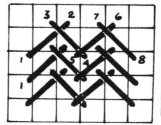

HERRINGBONE STITCH
(PLAITED STITCH).

Beading

Beadwork reached a zenith of popularity in the nineteenth century. At mid-century the beading usually was pastel in color and made of well-matched, carefully rounded beads. (This period corresponds to the peak period of American Indian beadwork.) Later the favorite colors were olive green, brown, gray, and red.

Parasol covers, pictures, and tea caddies were thread-counted in the same patterns that were used for Berlin wool work. These pieces carried on the tradition of the Stuart beaded baskets and looking-glass frames. Bellpulls, mantle covers, footstools, and fire screens were decorated with beading. The beads were worked onto tammy cloth or net, sewn on in strings or worked into cross stitches. In America beads were chiefly used, however, for woven, knitted, or crocheted purses or bags.

The glass tax was repealed in England in 1845. Prior to that time Venetian beads had cost five shillings an ounce. About 1854 large, cylindrical glass beads called O.P. beads were imported and were bought by the pound and used along with seed beads. Of the round beads no. 3 was the largest size and was used for crochet. No. 2 was used for cushions, table covers, and bags. No. 1 beads were used for clothing, small reticules, and netted articles. The beads were available in a wide range of shades, so it was possible to work out naturalistic effects. Steel beads were popular, but they were apt to rust.

Gem shades were the favorites: turquoise, amber, opal, emerald, and rose. During the height of Berlin wool work (about 1850) a type of needlework called German embroidery was popular. Typical floral designs were worked with a range of white to gray to black beads. The background was a brilliant color. Often the entire work was beaded, as in the bag shown in Plate 14.

VI Patchwork, Appliqué, and Quilting

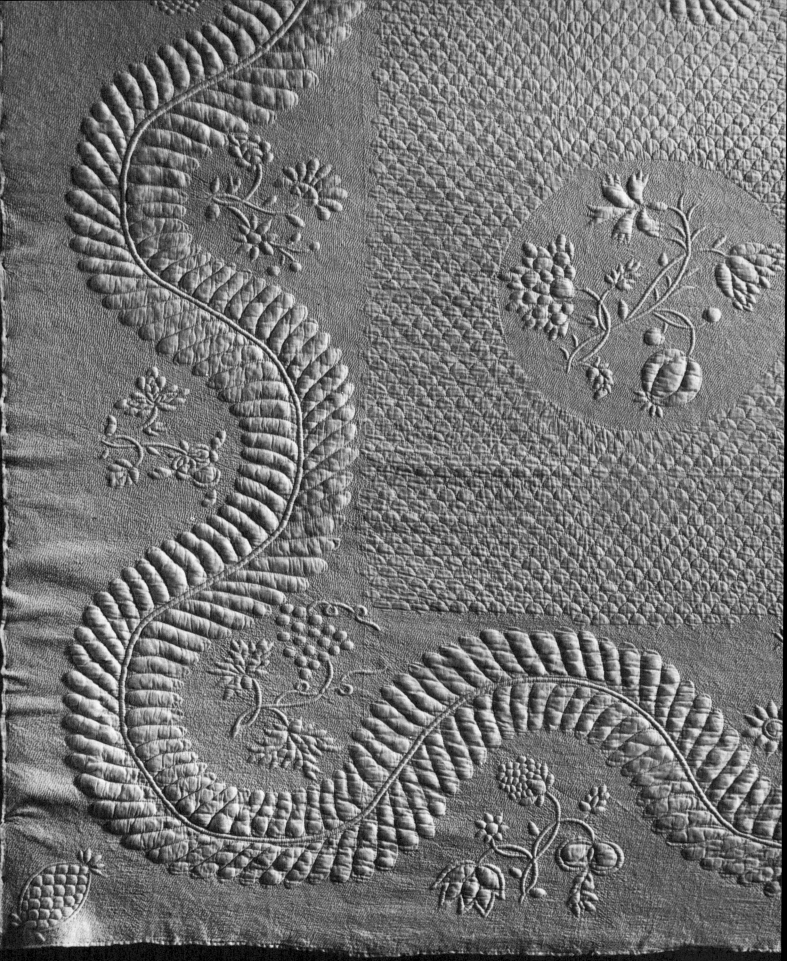

Patchwork, Appliqué, and Quilting

Coverlet of fine white cotton muslin with thin cotton batting interlining and linen backing. The larger motifs are stuffed from the back. 1800–20. Wadsworth Atheneum, lent by Mrs. Frederic J. Agate.

In the days before blankets and comforters were commercially manufactured, the making of bedclothing was a necessary household task. To meet the need, colonial women put together available materials, using a trio of methods that have become virtually inseparable: patchwork, appliqué, and quilting.

So closely associated are these techniques that the meanings of the terms have intermingled. We think of a pieced quilt as patchwork, while we call a patched quilt appliqué. The dictionary tells us that to piece means to add or attach, to unite or reunite parts or fragments into a whole. When we look up the definition for patch, we find that the repair, or adding on, function is primary. At the end of a list of definitions is "to make up of patches, as for a quilt." The origin of the word is uncertain. A century or more ago a glazed cotton fabric with printed designs, used to make counterpanes and bed hangings, sometimes appliquéd, was also called patch.

Quilt, as a term for bedcovering, was used in England. The Latin *culcita* means a stuffed sack or pillow or pad for a bed, and probably is the root of the fourteenth-century French word *cuilte*, which means the same. Coverlet, from the French *couvre-lit*, and encountered here earlier, now refers to an outer cover. Counterpane derives from the French *contrepoinct*, as we find in the 1650 edition of Randle Cotgrave's *Dictionarie of the French and English Tongues:*

> Contrepoinct: m. *The back stitch, or quilting stitch; also a quilt, counterpoint (quilted) covering; also a crossing, difference, opposition, also a ground, or plain-song (in Musick.)*

and:

> Contrepoincté: m. ée: f. *Quilted, wrought with the backe stitch; also interchanged, set backward and forward; crossed, stood against, or in opposition with.*
> l'ay la peau toute contrepoinctée de coups. *My skinne coat hath received as many knocks as a quilt hath stitches.*

Semiclassical scrolls for close-stitched, corded quilting.

Each of the three principal techniques used in making American stuffed bedcovers is of ancient origin. Quilting is an old art in Asia, North Africa, and Europe. It has been used in China for clothing and armor since the earliest times. Patchworks were made in Egypt and Persia. The famous appliqués of the Altai Mountain region, made by the Scythians, were used for wall hangings, horse gear, and clothing.

Quilting

When Dutch and English colonists set sail for the New World, quilting already had a long history. In Robin Hood's time English archers wore padded armor. In Caxton's edition of the *Morte Darthur*, printed in 1485, we find: "Thenne Balen loked in to a fayre litil gardyn, and vnder a laurel tre he sawe her lye vpon a quylt of grene samyte and a knyght in her armes fast halsynge eyther other and vnder their hedes grasse & herbes." In 1540 Catherine Howard, soon to be married to Henry VIII, received, as a royal compliment, twenty-three silk quilts. Listed in 1614 among the effects of Henry Howard, Earl of Northampton, was a "china quilte stiched in chequer worke with yealowe silk the grounde white." Fashionable eighteenth-century women wore warm quilted underskirts. There were other uses: in 1609 Ben Jonson wrote in *Epicoene; or, The Silent Woman*, "And you have fastened a thick quilt or flock bed on the outside of the door."

Some of the finest coverlets in the United States have neither piecing nor appliqué. Designs were achieved with quilting only. Among the earliest of these were coverlets made of linsey-woolsey, a type of cloth woven with a wool weft on a cotton or linen warp that originated in England in Lindsey, a village in Suffolk. (In early English inventories the name appears as lynsy wolsye.)

The raw materials for making linsey-woolsey were available in the colonies. Homespun linsey-woolsey found many uses. For bedcovers loom widths of the fabric were sewn together to make a piece wide enough to fit the bed. A linen piece also was prepared in the same size and the two cloths were stretched in a frame with a thin padding of wool between them. The layers were sewn together, usually with running stitches, following a pattern drawn on the top. Favorite designs were parallel lines, checks, geometric devices traced around a saucer or teacup, flowers, leaves, baskets, pineapples, and feathers. Blues, reds, and browns were the most popular colors for bedcovers, which often were glazed, an effect obtained by polishing the cloth by hand or by applying diluted gum arabic or egg white.

Traditional all-over quilting patterns.

Quilted silk bedcover. 1750–1800.
Museum of Fine Arts, Boston, gift
of Miss Emily Douglas Furness.

Waistcoat section of quilted linen. New England, 1725–50. Museum of Fine Arts, Boston, gift of the Misses Rose and Elizabeth Townsend.

Fragment of a petticoat owned and presumably made by Eunice Backus Trumbull, who married Jonathan Trumbull, Jr., governor of Connecticut 1796–1809. Calamanco lined with wool and backed with tabby-weave wool, ca. 1766. Wadsworth Atheneum, gift of the Estate of Miss Henrietta W. Hubbard through Miss Maria Trumbull Dana.

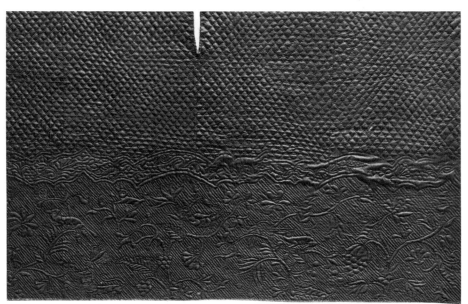

A few spreads were made in silk. At the Jeremiah Lee Mansion in Marblehead there is a silk cover quilted in feather patterns, probably made during the eighteenth century.

Quilted white linen coverlets also are seldom seen. White-on-white quilting was being done in England in the time of Queen Anne, and it was brought from there to the colonies. During the eighteenth century white coverlets were made of linen, but by the nineteenth century cotton was more common.

The principal difference between the linsey-woolsey and the all-white coverlets, aside from the degree of warmth, was in the manner of quilting. White padded quilts usually were made with some areas raised in greater relief than others, in a technique best known today as trapunto. To make the relief areas, the warps and wefts of a loosely-woven backing were spread apart and stuffing inserted between prestitched design outlines—work that can be done with a tapestry needle. When the wadding was in place, the backing threads were returned to position.

In England during the seventeenth century, quilting frequently was stitched with yellow silk thread, which also was used for additional embroidery. Similar quilting could be found in the colonies, often in clothing. The padding was a thick cord. Linen and silk dresses and waistcoats, as well as bed furnishings, were decorated

Pattern for corded quilting adapted from a silk petticoat in the Museum of Fine Arts, Boston. In the original the larger flowers are padded in relief.

with corded quilting. It seems probable that the quilting design was drawn on the top layer, then top and lining were joined with back or running stitches worked in parallel lines, making channels into which cords later could be inserted. The thick soft cords probably were threaded onto a blunt needle and inserted from the back, as in making trapunto. Or the design may have been traced on the lining and the cords tacked to it, and the outer layer then basted over backing and cords. Back stitches or running stitches would then have been worked closely on each side of the cords, causing them to stand out in relief.

In America before 1800, window hangings, heavy curtains, and chair seats and table covers, as well as bedcovers, were quilted, as were dresses, hoods, capes, petticoats, and waistcoats. Richly designed, quilted underskirts were worn with patterned chintz, brocaded, or crewel-embroidered overskirts. Intricate border patterns were combined with a powdering of small sprays on neat geometric grounds.

The scarcity of white bedcovers may be due to an early law forbidding the purchase of cotton cloth for this purpose and the difficulty of obtaining enough yardage of uniform whiteness to make a cover. The earliest beds, while short, were very wide, some-

Ship design developed as a motif for quilting.

times measuring more than 6 feet (to accommodate more than two people), and they were high, so coverlets had to be large. Some were high enough to house a trundle bed.

White quilts also required the most expert sewing. To bring out a design solely with the play of light and shadow requires very close stitching and makes necessary the tedious business of stuffing motifs individually. As a rule, these covers were most carefully designed, the drawing highly refined. A unique, outstanding example is the famous Secession Quilt made by Mrs. P. D. Cook of South Carolina, which shows cornucopias spilling pomegranates, grapes, and roses. The center symbol is an eagle on a starry firmament. The design of the inner square is filled out with floral garlands. The border shows the arms of South Carolina and portraits of three of its governors. There also are portraits of Washington and of Mrs. Cook's husband, a general, and the words "E Pluribus Unum" and "Secession—Yancey, 1860." Despite the disparity of its ornaments, the quilt has an elegant appearance. An article in the February 1929 issue of *Antiques* reports that this quilt was one of two that Mrs. Cook had made within a period of six months. The other unfortunately was destroyed.

Many of the patterns used for one-color quilts are familiar. The Shell, or Fish Scale, pattern appears on Oriental and medieval quilting, as well as on early English examples. Among the patterns that made their way from England to the colonies in the seventeenth century were: straight parallel line patterns; Single, Double, and Triple Diamonds; Hanging Diamonds, Inch Squares, Broken Plaids, Fans, Ocean Waves, and Twisted Ropes. Plate pattern (Pincushion, True Lover's Knot) appears on a quilt made in Marblehead in 1792. Single Feather, Double Feather, Pineapple, and Grape were American favorites. In the late eighteenth century stylized roses, violets, and tulips were used a great deal. Hearts, usually reserved for brides' quilts, were considered an evil omen when used elsewhere.

Many of the designs used for quilting look a great deal like those used for embroidery, and no doubt the same patterns were used for both. In addition to the grounding patterns already mentioned, others used were: Diagonal, Cross Bar, Horizontal, Basket Weave, and Splint. Pictorial motifs similar to those used for embroidery or appliqué were: Tree of Life (later Weeping Willow), Cornucopia, Star and Crown, Pineapple, Dove of Peace, American Eagle, Prince's Feather (or Princess Feather), Feather Wreath, Wheel of Fortune, Acanthus, Rope, Maltese Cross, Oak Leaf, Fan, Peacock Fan, Basket, Star, Starfish, Teacup, and Running Vine.

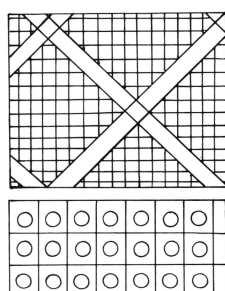

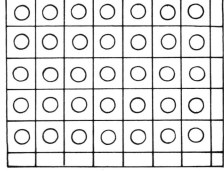

Traditional all-over quilting patterns.

"Pine Apples." Illustration from Crispijn van de Passe's *Hortus Floridus*.

Traditional all-over quilting patterns.

Also, Bellflower, Conventional Rose, Persian Pear, Pickle, Daisy, Daylily, Ragged Robin, Heart, Swirl, Serpentine, Widening Circles, Ocean Wave, Crescent, Clamshell, Spider Web, Indian Hatchet, Sausage Chain, Slave Chain, Tide Mill (Mill Wheel).

The pineapple was a favorite motif for quilting. The tulip craze of the seventeenth century, which had almost brought economic ruin to the Netherlands, gave way to a vogue for pineapples in the eighteenth. André Thevet, a monk, had introduced pineapples to Europe in 1555. In 1720 in England Henry Tellende, Sir Matthew Decker's botanist, grew one, and by 1730 the pineapple fad was well under way. By the nineteenth century the pineapple had become a symbol of perfection, and an established emblem of hospitality as well. It appears in many needleworks and was especially popular for quilting.

When the eagle was adopted for the Great Seal of the United States, in 1782, it set off another craze. The motif was painted, carved, engraved, stenciled, and embroidered on all sorts of objects, and frequently appears in quilting.

Other symbols were picked up from furniture ornaments. These included shells, frets, and fluted columns, which, in the hands of furniture makers less skilled than, for example, those of Newport, had deteriorated into simpler motifs. Shells flattened to fans; rosettes became pinwheels.

For identification, American quilts sometimes are classified by the period during which they were made. Thus, quilts from before the Revolution are called colonial, and those made during what was the neoclassical period in Europe are referred to as empire quilts. Pioneer quilts appeared after 1840. Those made during the 1850s and 1860s may be called Civil War quilts. From 1876 until about 1896 centennial quilts were popular. Some quilts made after 1840 are called Victorian.

American quilts made before 1750 are notable because of their rarity but a great many made in the next hundred years have survived. Early quilts usually were square. A typical composition consisted of four blocks 1 yard square with an 18-inch border all around, making a huge quilt on which very large patterns could be used. Quilts made with smaller blocks were a later innovation. The number of pieces in a quilt always has been a subject for admiration, as has the closeness of the rows of quilting. Twelve thousand yards of quilting stitches may be required to finish a fine quilt.

Aside from the technical differences between pieced, appliquéd, and other types of bedcovers, there are regional differences in style. In the early days in New England quilts were relatively

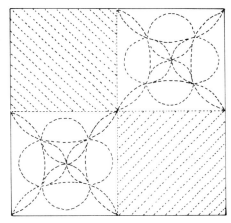

Overlapping circle motif for quilting square blocks.

Quilting border patterns.

232

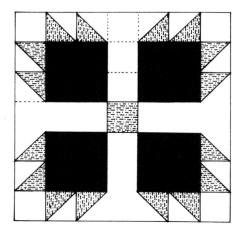

Bear's Paw.

restrained in design and usually not elaborately quilted. Pennsylvania quilts, on the other hand, were boldly designed and involved a great deal of expert sewing. The bedcovers of the South were delicately designed and embroidered, and minutely quilted, reflecting the presence of slave labor.

With the pioneer movement westward, regional variations blurred. A traditionalism developed which parallels that of Eastern Europe: designs were transmitted from mother to daughter and from neighbor to neighbor. Women copied patterns so often that some designs gained a certain fame. But although the pattern might stay the same, the name often changed. Long Island's Duck Feet in the Mud, Pennsylvania's Hand of Friendship, and Ohio's Bear's Paw are all the same design.

Pennsylvania German needlewomen did not shrink from difficult sewing feats. They not only executed elaborate designs like Full-Blown Tulip (Dutch Tulip) and Star and Crescent (Twinkling Star), pieceworks full of intricate curves, but also cut lozenge-shaped pieces on the bias, which made the joining more difficult. They quilted these demanding patterns precisely, using tiny stitches.

Southern quilts are restrained and elegant in design. Many of them combine piecing and appliqué on a white ground. Beautifully printed imported chintzes were available for quilt makers, and there were skilled American printers, like John Hewson, who contributed exquisite printed cottons. Motifs from these handsome chintzes were cut out and applied to the quilts. Often the edges of the appliqués were buttonholed with tiny stitches in silk thread, usually yellow. Stems and other details were added in embroidery. Bands of geometric pieced designs made of calico separated the major areas of the composition. A fine example is the coverlet owned at present by Ann Kimbrough Brown McIlhenny, daughter of Dr. Murray Brown, former health commissioner of the city of Chicago, who has provided the details of its history.

Motifs from chintz and printed cottons appliquéd on a coverlet dated 1782. Details are embroidered. Henry Francis du Pont Winterthur Museum.

Appliqué and embroidery coverlet
made by Sarah Furman Warner,
Greenfield Hill, Connecticut, ca.
1800. Greenfield Village and Henry
Ford Museum.

The genealogy of this Framed Medallion quilt, which was made by a Brown family ancestor, Jane Warwick, and is dated 1795, is unusually complete. All its owners lived in the Appalachian Mountains, in the area between what is now Bath County, Virginia, and Pocahontas and Greenbrier counties in West Virginia. The quilt was handed down through the family as follows:

Jacob Warwick   m.   Mary Vance

Jane Warwick, the quilt maker and second wife of
William Travers Gatewood

Thomas Gatewood (son by first wife)   m.   Nancy Warwick

Andrew Gatewood   m.   Sallye Moffett

Hannah Moffett Gatewood   m.   John Woods Warwick (probably Jacob's great-grandson)

Sallye Gatewood Warwick   m.   John Ligon

Mary Louisa Ligon   m.   Julius Jackson Coyner

Louise Jackson Coyner   m.   Murray Cox Brown

Ann Kimbrough Brown   m.   John Boyd McIlhenny

T-Blocks.

Indian Trail.

Dr. Brown owns a farm alongside Jacob Warwick's original grant of 44,000 acres near the Greenbrier River. Life in this isolated country was in sharp contrast to that in the slaveholding plantation country along the James River, where other quilts were made, al-

Joseph's Coat (Scrap Bag).

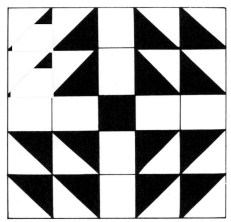

Handy Andy (one version).

though the family did have a limited number of slaves. (The last one died during the lifetime of Dr. Brown's first wife, Louise Coyner Brown, and is buried on their farm.) There was no water route to the east, but primitive roads through the Alleghenies led to the north-south board road laid out in the Shenandoah Valley by George Washington, and gaps in the Blue Ridge Mountains permitted communication eastward with the coastal regions.

How the cloth to make the appliqués on the Brown family Medallion quilt ever got to the back country is not known, but Dr. Brown's guess is that "a bolt of cloth from Europe for a lady's dress was just the thing to put in your saddlebag when you had been away from your lady on a short trip of one month." In some such manner, printed fabrics did make their way into remote areas, and their remnants were preserved in quilts and coverlets long after the garments for which they were intended had been worn to shreds.

Southern coverlets were exquisite tours de force of the quilt maker's art. The professionalism with which they were embroidered and quilted made them perfectly appropriate for the formal settings of fine Southern homes. (Prime examples, the Westover-Berkeley coverlet and the Hillsborough Plantation cover, can be seen at the Valentine Museum, Richmond, Virginia.)

In American quilts the usual filling is cotton, which has been grown in this country since 1621, although not widely until 1760. Sometimes cast-off garments were shredded for quilt stuffing, but this is apt to be lumpy. After 1792 cotton was mechanically ginned to eliminate the seeds. Earlier, busy Northern housewives frequently did not remove all the seeds. In the South, where slave hands were available for such work, quilts were filled with cotton that was seedless. The first cotton gin left two or three seeds every few inches. Later improvements made the filling more seed free, but quilts made with filling picked clean of seeds by expert slave hands were the most seed free of all.

Fine quilts were not used every day, but were saved for special occasions. Distinguished guests, such as the circuit-riding minister or a dignitary of the church, were favored with the best quilt, which probably was appliquéd and had a splendidly quilted background of new matching cloth. Appliquéd quilts were the most carefully protected and so have survived in greater numbers than other types of quilts.

Special black and white quilts were made to be used on occasions of mourning. One Kentucky quilt has a center medallion onto which were stitched motifs of coffins, one for each deceased member of the family.

Coverlet inscribed P W made by Ann Walgrave Warner (1758–1826) for Phebe Warner (?) of block-printed cottons with East Indian motifs, appliquéd and embroidered on linen. New York, ca. 1800. Metropolitan Museum of Art, gift of Catherine E. Cotheal, 1938.

Star and Crescent (Twinkling Star).

Star of the West (Compass, Four Winds).

A complete dower chest contained twelve quilts for everyday use and one especially lovely "bride's quilt." The most expensive part of quilt making came when filling and backing had to be purchased, so until there was need for them, the completed tops were stored away, awaiting the time when their maker became engaged. When a wedding date finally was set, friends came to help finish the quilts. Sending out invitations to a quilting bee was tantamount to announcing an engagement.

Apparently there were no fixed rules of etiquette governing the quilting bee. Some accounts report that guests arrived at five or six in the morning, sometimes at two in the afternoon. In the Harriet Beecher Stowe story "The Minister's Wooing," guests arrive at the party at two o'clock with food and drink: hyson tea, pound cake, pie, doughnuts, cheese, and cold meat.

Sometimes the design already was drawn on the quilt when the women came; sometimes they collaborated in setting up and marking the design. There seems to have been a standard procedure when the day ended. The men came in, and there was a large meal, then merriment, dancing, and games, depending on the moral temper and the religious convictions of the community involved.

238

Album quilt, possibly a friendship
or wedding quilt. Appliquéd cotton.
Helen Louise Allen Textile
Collection, University of Wisconsin.

Floral Medallion coverlet, 1830–35,
said to have belonged to Elizabeth
Patterson, who married Jerome
Bonaparte in Baltimore, Maryland,
in 1803. English block-printed
chintz motifs appliquéd on muslin
with quilting in elaborate patterns.
Art Institute of Chicago, gift of
Mrs. Jennie Hodge Schmidt.

Log Cabin bedspread. Silk, with
bobbin lace border. Late nineteenth
century. Art Institute of Chicago,
gift of Mrs. Charles S. Dewey, Jr.

Job's Tears.

Between six and twelve women could sit at a quilting frame.
We are told that one top would not occupy enough women to make
a party, so quilting bees were not arranged until at least two tops
were complete and ready for quilting. Sometimes the bee was held
at the same time as a barn-raising, apple paring, or cornhusking.
It was a welcome event for people who lived on farms at a distance
from one another.

Mrs. John A. Logan, wife of a Civil War general, tells in
Reminiscences of a Soldier's Wife how things were done at a quilting bee in southern Illinois in 1840. The quilt lining was laced into
the frame and cotton filling was laid carefully over it; then the top
was positioned over it. When all the parts of the quilt were in place,
they were carefully basted together along the edges. A chalk line
was used in marking the pattern. Fan patterns were most popular
at the time. After two or more rows of fans were made, the frame
was loosened and the finished portion rolled up. Then the frame
was repegged and the process was repeated. Women who did not
like to sew could find plenty to do in the kitchen until, as in the
words of the old song, it was time for "seeing Nellie home."

Since first-rate quilts obviously took months to finish, one
questions whether truly fine quilts could have been produced at

quilting bees. There is no doubt that in most quilts the major part of the labor is in the quilting, and that the quilting requires the most skill. Even with twelve workers arriving at five in the morning, it is unlikely that a quilting pattern with any appreciable degree of elaboration could be finished in one day. Certainly the women would have been too exhausted for any revelry afterward. The gossip and chatting that allegedly went on do not suggest undue concentration on work, and work time must have been shortened a good deal by the lengthy luncheon. On top of that we are told that the work day stopped before five for supper preparation.

So we have to believe that quilting often was done by one woman alone. Usually tops were made in winter; quilting was done in the summer. To have a quilting frame set up in the house during the winter meant crowding the space around the fireplace. Quilting had to be done in the kitchen or some other warm room to keep fingers from stiffening in the cold. Many homes had only one fireplace, so a quilting frame in use during the winter was a nuisance that had to be moved constantly. When not in use, it was propped against a wall or put out of the way elsewhere.

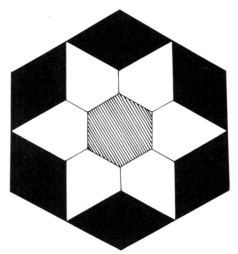

Rising Star (one version).

Patchwork

The first American quilts, strictly utilitarian, were pieced together from scraps and remnants. During the early years in colonial America all cloth was imported, and it was very expensive. Patched clothing was welcomed; a patch meant extra warmth, but even patched clothing eventually went into the scrap bag. Out of remaining usable parts quilts were made. Most of these were woolen covers of the crazy-quilt variety, but simple patterns began to be made very early. Hit and Miss was a pattern using small rectangles, the final design depending upon the arrangement of light and dark pieces. Purely functional bedcovers of this type were made for a long period; they can be seen in the small, austere homes that accurately preserve the quality of life at New Salem, Illinois, where Abraham Lincoln lived from 1831 until 1837.

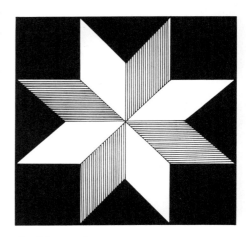

Le Moyne Star.

Some of the early quilts made from castoffs and remnants are quite gay. Old reds did a great deal to brighten color schemes. Certain patterns, like Log Cabin (which can be made from oddly assorted scraps), have a key piece, and often the most brilliant color was saved for this piece.

Many beautiful quilts were made using Log Cabin, Mosaic, Roman Stripe, Roman Square, Brick Wall, Streak of Lightning, and similar patterns in which cloth pieces did not have to match and many remnants could be used up. The purely abstract con-

Dutchman's Puzzle.

Yankee Puzzle.

Windmill (Water Wheel, Mill Wheel).

Pieced patchwork cushion in Flower Basket design worked by Sylvia Roe Bath. Trial quilt blocks make fine pillow covers.

Pinwheels. 1855. Courtesy Rhea
Goodman, New York.

243

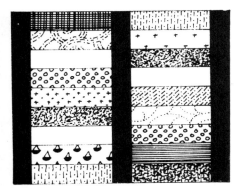

Roman Stripe.

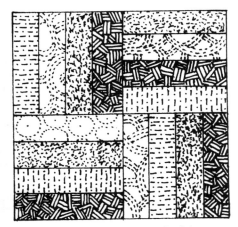

Roman Square (Roman Block).

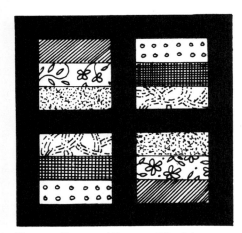

Roman Square (Roman Block).

244

siderations of color, texture, and shape that went into the planning of these quilts often resulted in sophisticated, highly creative designs.

Roman Stripe was made by joining light and dark strips of cloth of various widths, long sides of the scraps abutting into one long strip. These strips, after trimming, were sewed together with a plain band, usually black, between them.

In making Roman Square (or Roman Block), three strips of color were joined, sandwich fashion, to make a square block. (This can be called a three-patch block; four- and nine-patch blocks are the backbone of patchwork quilting.) As a rule, the individual squares are assembled with bands of plain color between them.

Brick Wall, predictably, has rectangles placed in successive rows so that vertical seams in one row occur halfway between the vertical seams in the adjacent rows. Light and dark arrangements can be worked out so that a variety of patterns emerge.

Mosaic also can be made in various designs. Also called Honeycomb and Grandmother's Flower Garden, this design is composed of hexagons. Its patterns are achieved through the arrangement of light and dark pieces, often with an almost incredible number of pieces measuring as small as ½ or ⅝ inch.

Log Cabin is one of the most interesting quilt patterns and certainly one of the most popular. It can be arranged in many striking variations, some of which have their own names: Barn-Raising, Windmill Blades, Courthouse Steps. The basic Log Cabin block has a small square in the center. Around this piece four narrow strips are placed generally in swastika arrangement. Usually two are dark, two light. Additional strips are added until the block has reached the desired size. One-half the block, then, is dark; one-half is light. The blocks are arranged so that light and dark areas abut in various ways to form concentric diamonds (Barn-Raising), long diagonal zigzags, or checkerboards. When light strips are placed opposite one another, instead of at right angles, checkered patterns emerge. Courthouse Steps is one of these, but in making blocks for this design, the strips in each round are of two lengths. The two longer strips are placed on opposite sides of the center square, at right angles to the two short strips.

In some superb coverlets of the Log Cabin variety hexagonal rather than square blocks are prepared, starting with a small hexagon as the center piece.

More than half the patterns for patchwork coverlets are based on the so-called four-patch design, a pattern that begins with the division of the basic block into four smaller squares of equal size.

Log Cabin blocks joined to make the
Barn-Raising pattern.

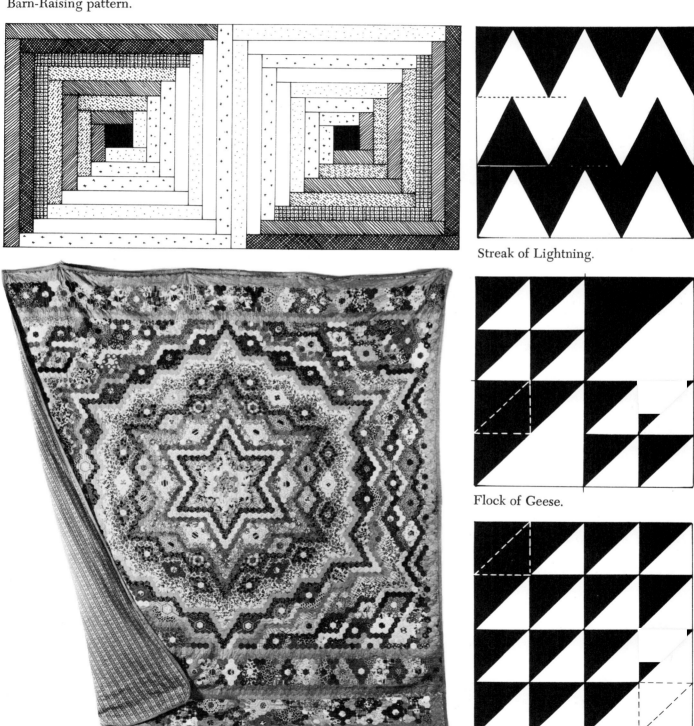

Streak of Lightning.

Flock of Geese.

Quilt in Mosaic or Grandmother's
Flower Garden pattern. Ca. 1850.
Greenfield Village and Henry Ford
Museum.

Hovering Hawks (one version).

Civil War album quilt. Pieced flag in the center has wool-embroidered stars. Separately made blocks were quilted, bound in white, and joined. Messages, verses, and Biblical quotations are written in ink on some of the plain squares. Granville, New York, during or immediately after the Civil War. Wadsworth Atheneum, gift of Mrs. Emerson G. Taylor.

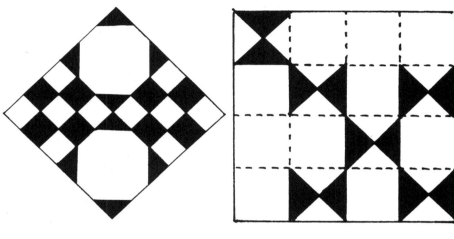

Snowball (left) and Circus Clowns (right), two simple designs that are superb when repeated.

Circular Saw.

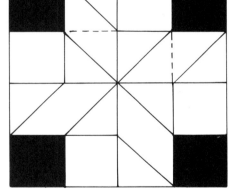

Henry Clay's Choice.

Pineapple (Maltese Cross).

Each (or some) of these squares may be composed of even smaller pieces. Patterns within each of the smaller squares may differ, but often there are two subpatterns, each used for two squares.

Nine-patch blocks can be very intricate. Occasionally, all nine patches that make up the block are also pieced. The designs of nine-patch blocks sometimes are superbly conceived. Circular Saw and Diamond and Star, shown here and on page 251, are two surprising versions of the nine-patch block, but neither is necessarily a nine-patch. They can be cut and assembled differently, if desired.

Many patchwork designs that appear at first glance to be made up of odd-shaped pieces intricately joined are really simply combinations of squares and triangles assembled in blocks in the usual ways. Dotted lines in the pattern drawings in this book suggest possible methods of construction.

Flyfoot (Devil's Puzzle).

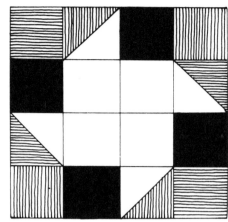

Pinwheel (one version).

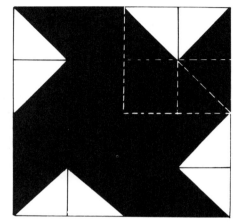

Churn Dash.

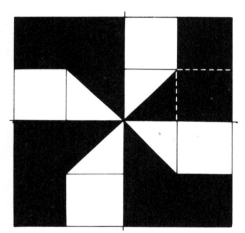

Nelson's Victory.

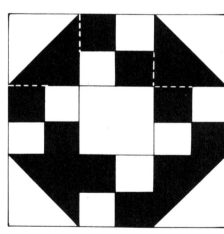

Prairie Queen (one version).

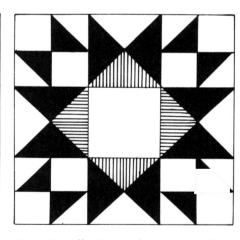

King David's Crown (one version).

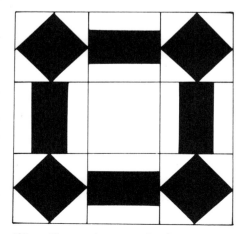

Kitty Corner (one version).

Winged Square.

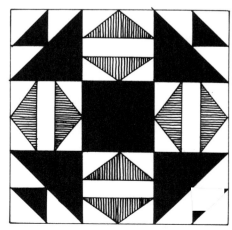

Joseph's Coat (one version). See also page 236.

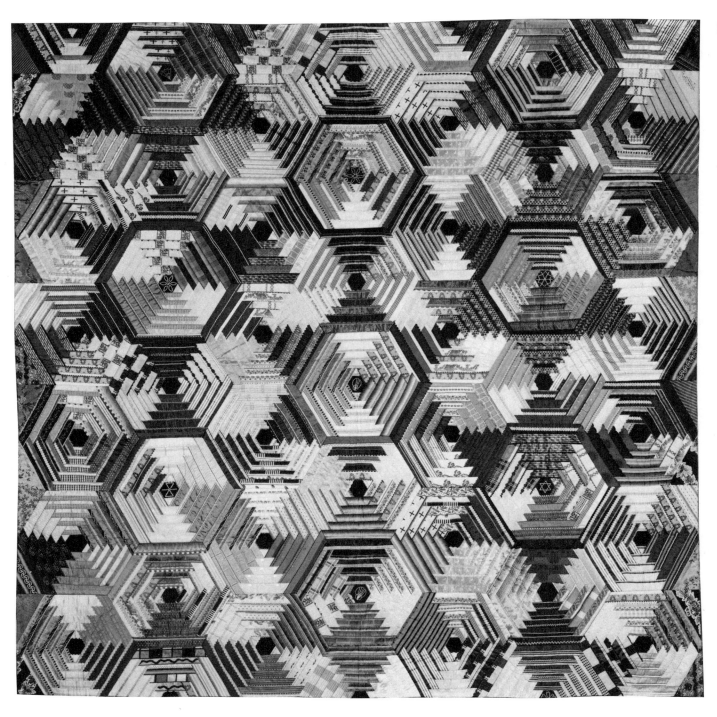

Variation of Log Cabin pattern
pieced in silk. West Gardiner,
Maine, ca. 1890. Philadelphia
Museum of Art, gift of Miss
Harriet Plimpton.

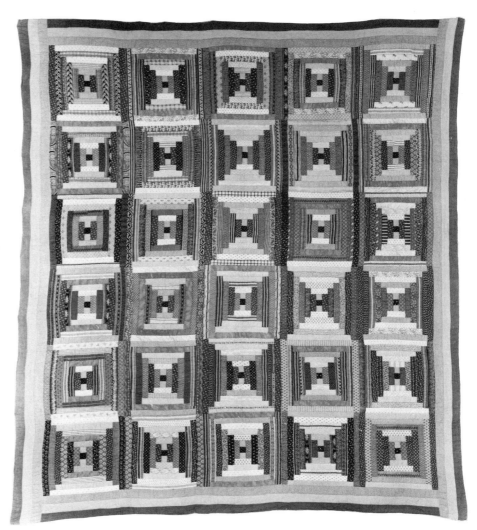

250   Courthouse Steps pattern pieced in cotton. Pennsylvania, ca. 1860. Courtesy Rhea Goodman, New York.

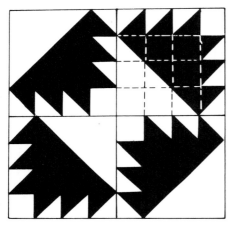

Barrister's Block (Lawyer's Puzzle).

Fox and Geese (Crosses and Losses).

Quilts made with great eight-pointed stars or suns as a central medallion are among the most numerous of those preserved from early times. The patterns are known by a variety of names, but their construction (from lozenge-, or diamond-shaped, pieces) is basically the same. Star of Bethlehem, Star of the East, Texas Star, Lone Star, Beautiful Star, Morning Star, Evening Star, and the small Le Moyne Star or Lemon Star are some of the names associated with the star designs. Sunburst, or Rising Sun, patterns are essentially the same, except that the figure is filled out to make an octagon, rather than arranged in eight points. In many quilts the great centered figure spreads out to reach the borders of the coverlet. An eight-foot star may have eight hundred or more pieces and two thousand yards of quilting stitches. Quilts this size were made for the large beds of the eighteenth century. By 1812 the three-quarter bed was popular, and quilts were much smaller, with the scale of the quilt blocks proportionately reduced.

Old quilts with six-pointed great stars are rare, indicating that the pattern was not widely used, possibly because the irregular background presents design problems and the star appears ungainly when extended to a very large size. Eight-pointed stars fit

Detail of a Lone Star quilt pieced by **251** Mrs. Almira Dudley Clay. The full composition includes nine stars. Ca. 1830. Art Institute of Chicago, gift of Mrs. William Burson.

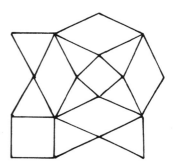

Diamond and Star can be made as a nine-patch or assembled from squares, triangles, and lozenges. For nine-patch, cut squares and triangles only, as shown in the outline drawing. No matter where the pattern is stopped, an attractive border appears and lends itself easily to combination with other patterns and colors for devising borders.

Variable Star (Ohio Star).

Dolly Madison Star.

Chicago Star.

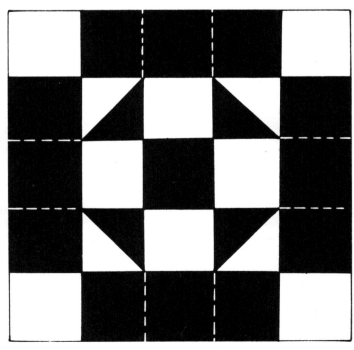

Philadelphia Pavement groups
squares around a nine-patch block.

Queen Charlotte's Crown (Indian Meadow).

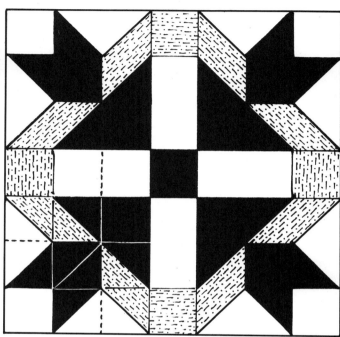

David and Goliath.

Northwest Star.

Falling Star.

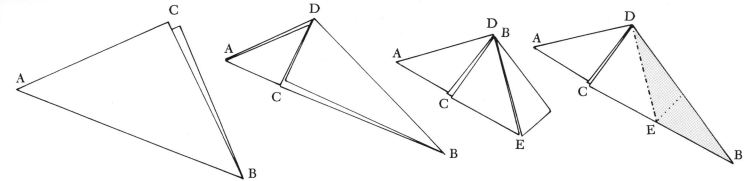

254

To make a template for the diamonds of an eight-pointed star:

1. Fold a square piece of paper diagonally to make a triangle.

2. Bring point C over to the fold line so that edges C-B are parallel to the fold line, making new fold B-D.

3. Bring point B up to point D to establish point E.

4. Cut through the layers of paper along line D-E. Shaded area B-D-E, opened out, reveals two joined diamonds. Cut along fold line B-E, which joins them, and you have two paper patterns from which templates can be made. A 6-by-6-inch square will produce diamonds approximately 2¾ by 6¼ inches. An 8-by-8-inch square makes diamonds about 3½ by 8½ inches. When cutting cloth pieces, remember to add a sufficient seam margin all the way around.

neatly into a square, leaving a "background" of four squares and four triangles. Lozenges with the necessary 45-degree and 135-degree angles may be made by the simple folding method shown here. While diamonds for a six-pointed star can also be made by a fold-and-cut method, it is difficult to achieve accuracy this way. A pattern drawn with a ruler as described in the second diagram is more precise.

Diamond star and Sunburst patterns are worked outward from a central star. Usually the second row of an eight-pointed-star design consists of sixteen diamonds of a different shade, two being set between each of the points of the original star. Occasionally, the second row of color consists of twenty-four diamonds, as shown in the shaded area of the Star of Bethlehem drawing, but this bold pattern is not seen often. Usually, the twenty-four-unit row is the third one, and the effect is softer because the colors mingle more gracefully.

To make a Sunburst pattern, one point of the initial eight-pointed star must point toward the top center of the cover, if the four sides of the resulting octagon are to line up with the four sides of the quilt and leave four triangles in the corners. Concentric rows of diamonds are then placed around the central star and are continued to the outer limits of the octagon.

To make a quilt with a large eight-pointed star, two star tips should point toward each side of the quilt ground. At first, concentric rows are added as for a Sunburst, but at some spot (depending on the desired size of the star) one of the concentric rows is interrupted by dropping out of the sequence the two diamonds of the same color that meet side by side (instead of point to point) and form the spokes radiating from the inner angles of the central star. From then on only the spaces between the remaining diamond points are filled in. In each succeeding row the number of spaces is consequently diminished, thus gradually narrowing the rows to points. To determine when to start decreasing the rows to make the points, plot the design in a scale drawing on paper first.

In old quilts the squares and triangles of the background of a star quilt sometimes were embellished with smaller stars, usually Le Moyne Stars (see Plate 20). Other quilts have botanical motifs cut from chintz and appliquéd into those areas, or the background may be plain but enriched with fancy quilting designs. The edges may be bordered or simply bound.

One interesting variation of the diamond-star pattern is Broken Star. A plain square is set between each of the points of a central star. Motifs identical to those of the original star are then

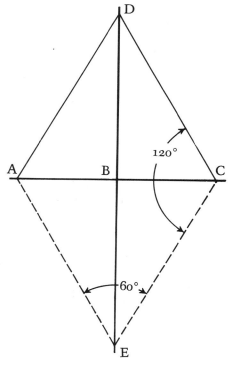

Sunburst design. Ca. 1840. Courtesy Rhea Goodman, New York.

255

Make a diamond (lozenge shape) for a six-pointed star by setting two equilateral triangles base to base. To make equilateral triangles, draw a straight horizontal line. Along this line, measure off a distance (A to C) with its midpoint at B. Draw a vertical line through point B, and at right angles to A-C. From point A draw a line equal in length to line A-C diagonally upward to where it will intersect line D-E. Draw another line of equal length diagonally from C to meet line D-E, forming triangle A-C-D. To complete the diamond, repeat the process below the horizontal line, forming triangle A-E-C and diamond A-D-C-E. Six equilateral triangles set point to point instead of base to base will form a hexagon.

Broken Star.

Slashed Star.

Caesar's Crown.

Full-Blown Tulip (Dutch Tulip).

Clamshell.

Ozark Diamond (Ozark Star).

Prairie Star (Harvest Sun, Ship's Wheel).

St. Louis Star (one version).

California Star (one version).

Star of Bethlehem (one version; also called Patty's Star).

258

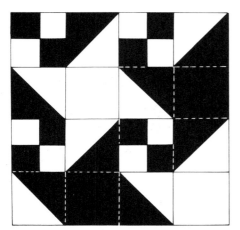

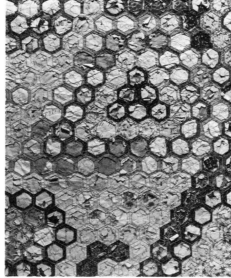

Detail of back of quilt showing paper templates still basted in place.

Unfinished English calico quilt in Honeycomb pattern. Ca. 1830. Art Institute of Chicago, gift of Robert G. Robinson.

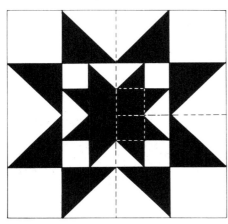

Two intricate four-patch blocks: Indiana Puzzle and Rising Star (Stars and Squares). Assemble sixteen, then four, blocks.

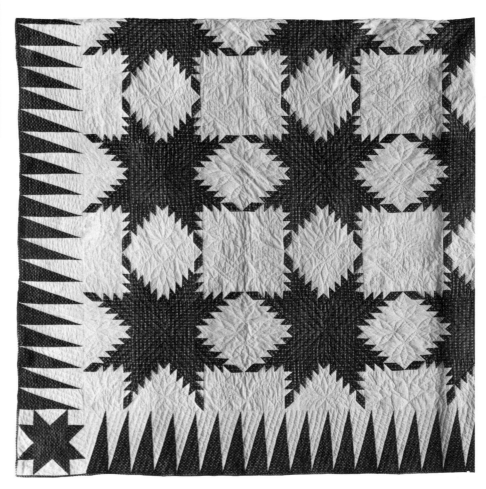

Feathered Star quilt pieced by Miss Ann Jennet Mitchell (b. 1814). South Britain, Connecticut, 1830–40. Wadsworth Atheneum, gift of Miss Ruth Mitchell.

placed around these squares, as shown in the drawing. To fill out the overall square design, three squares the same size as those around the center star are added to each corner, and two triangles to each side. The diagram shows the general arrangement of the pattern, but some actual quilts have many more rows of diamonds than this.

Stars may be made with forms other than lozenges. Some eight-pointed stars are composed of squares and triangles, in many variations and often with a saw-toothed edge, a feature that has given this pattern category one of its several names: Feathered Star. The feathered edge is achieved by outlining the star with small triangles as shown in the diagrams for Feathered Star and California Star. This pattern calls for careful piecing. The quilts tend to be delicate and intricate, in contrast to the boldness and large scale that characterize most of the Star of Bethlehem quilts.

Large stars are also a feature of many mosaiclike Honeycomb quilts composed of hexagonal pieces. Other stars introduce additional forms. The dominant shapes in pieced quilts are squares, rectangles, triangles, lozenges (diamonds), hexagons, and rhomboids. The diamond shapes used to make stars are also employed, either alone or in combination with squares, in the popular design known as Boxes, Baby Blocks, Stair Steps, Illusion, or Cube Work, and are found in other designs as well.

Shapes that are difficult to join, such as isosceles triangles with their bases altered into concave or convex arcs, and circles, half circles, and crescents, occur infrequently in pieced quilts. Clamshell, a pattern made entirely with curved seams, ceased to be made at the end of the eighteenth century.

Among the most intriguing pieced-work patterns are the reciprocal designs—those in which the limits of the background and of the individual blocks are ambiguous. Two such designs are Robbing Peter to Pay Paul (or Orange Peel) and Hearts and Gizzards (Pierre's Pompon). Some, like Drunkard's Path (also called Rocky Road to Dublin, Rocky Road to California, or Country Husband) and Fool's Puzzle, combine straight and curved seams. Indiana Puzzle is a clever sixteen-patch, or complex four-patch.

There are, of course, literally hundreds of patterns for patchwork quilts, the great majority of which can be interpreted as either four- or nine-patch arrangements. Increasing the nine-patch arrangement by another row of squares in each direction means dealing with sixteen squares, which is a more unwieldy number. Nine-patch, as examples demonstrate, can be complicated enough.

Baby Blocks.

Boxes.

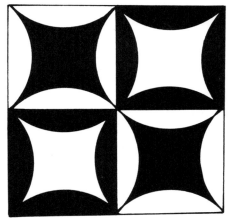

Robbing Peter to Pay Paul (one version).

260 Dutch Rose (Octagonal Star).

Georgetown Circle (Crown of
Thorns, Wedding Ring).

Christmas Star.

Mariner's Compass (Rising Star).

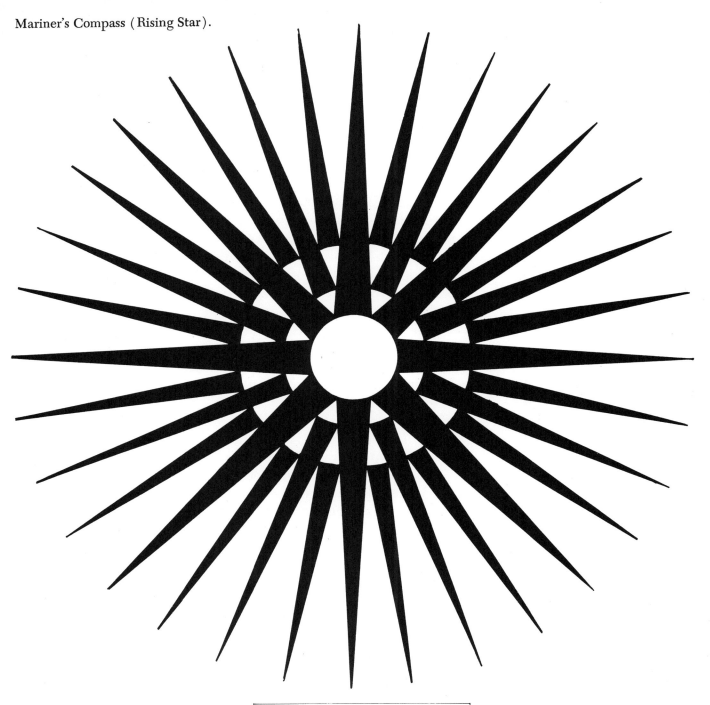

Blazing Star (one version).

Pine Tree (Temperance Tree).

Tree of Paradise.

Tree of Life (Christmas Tree).

262

Irish Chain is one of the simplest and best-known of the nine-patch designs. Nine squares of equal size are assembled in checkerboard fashion. Four of the squares are plain and five are composed of nine smaller squares in two colors, one of which is usually the same color as the larger plain squares. In assembling the quilt the large nine-patch blocks are alternated with plain blocks of the same size, linking the small squares in a diagonally crisscrossed pattern. When the coverlet is quilted, the plain blocks are usually treated to fancy designs.

Pine Tree pattern was popular everywhere. The motif had appeared on the Massachusetts Pine Tree shilling of 1652, and during the Revolutionary period it was displayed on the Continental flag, naval flags, and the flags of separate colonies. The pine tree is still featured on many state flags.

Tree patterns may be worked as blocks, as shown in the diagram of Tree of Life. Tree of Paradise groups small four-patch blocks into a larger twenty-five-patch block.

Ohio's Bear's Paw, as previously noted, was known by different names in different parts of the country. This was true of many patterns. Indian Trail also was known as Forest Path, Winding Walk, Rambling Road, Rambling Rose, Climbing Rose, Old Maid's Ramble, Storm at Sea, Flying Dutchman, North Wind, Weather Vane, Tangled Tares, Prickly Pear, and Irish Puzzle. And some names, such as Rising Star, have been applied to more than one pattern.

Superstitions attached to some patterns. Wandering Foot design was not used for children's beds. It was also considered unwise to use it on a young man's bed, and it certainly would not do as a bride's quilt. Some sought to ameliorate the curse by changing the name. Wandering Foot is now frequently known as Turkey Tracks, or Squares and Swallows, or Pincushion and Burrs. Piecing its curved seams makes this one of the more demanding patterns. Henry Clay's Choice is also known as Harry's Star, Henry of the West, Star of the West. Double Monkey Wrench has been called Love Knot, Hole-in-the-Barn Door, Puss in the Corner, Shoo-Fly, Lincoln's Platform, and Sherman's March.

Until the pioneer period, local characteristics were marked. Pictorial motifs like Pine Tree originated in New England, but also were used in the South. The Pennsylvania Germans worked conventionalized motifs in patterns full of circles and arcs.

There were a great number of themes among the patterns, including religion, politics, recreation, and occupations. Some patterns honored individuals. Le Moyne Star was named for Pierre

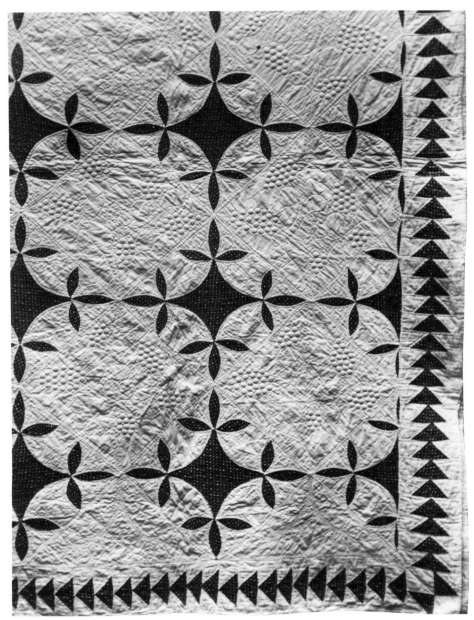

Drunkard's Path.

Fool's Puzzle.

Wandering Foot or Turkey Tracks (detail). Pieced blocks alternate with plain blocks quilted in grapevine pattern, the grapes stuffed to stand out in relief. Wild Goose Chase border. Nineteenth century, about 1830. Art Institute of Chicago. Gift of Mrs. Emma B. Hodge.

264 Coverlet signed by Esther S. Bradford. Dated 1807. Inscriptions read: "Truth is the Summum Bonum," "Let the Arms of America Be Subjugated Only to the Banners of the Cross and the Sweet Servitude of Immanuel. His Yoke is Easy & His Burden Light." Montville, Connecticut. Greenfield Village and Henry Ford Museum.

Pineapple.

Lady Fingers and Sunflowers.

Flower Garden quilt of four appliquéd squares plus border. Probably late nineteenth century. Wadsworth Atheneum, gift of Miss Vivian L. Beach.

le Moyne, Sieur d'Iberville, who led the colonization of Louisiana, and his brother, Jean Baptiste le Moyne, Sieur de Bienville, who founded New Orleans in 1718. There were Biblical names, such as David and Goliath, which is also known as Four Darts, Bull's Eye, Flying Darts, and Doe and Darts. The pattern called Job's Tears in 1800 acquired names that mark the course of history: Slave Chain (1825), Texas Tears (1840), Rocky Road, Kansas Troubles (post–Civil War), and Endless Chain.

Appliqué

Unlike piecing, which is at its best in nonobjective designs, appliqué almost always has been used for natural, but somewhat conventionalized forms. The felt examples of Pazyryk, the Altai Mountain region of southern Siberia, dating fifth century before Christ, are the oldest, and among the finest, appliqués that exist. In the low-ceilinged burial pits, or kurgans, of the region lay well-embalmed bodies fully equipped for future life. The walls of the chamber were covered all around with hangings of felt appliqué, too large to be carried up small entry passages by looters. Undisturbed in the constantly frozen pits, the felts were well preserved. The designs of the hangings, and of saddle trappings on horses buried just outside the walls of the chambers, showed goddesses, horsemen, and griffins in shades of red, yellow, blue, black, and beige. Some of the appliqué is neatly overcast into place; some of it has couched cording over the edges.

In the seventeenth century, Turkish war tents, decorated richly with appliquéd and embroidered flowers, were taken as booty to Western Europe, where they must have stirred interest in the appliqué technique. Eastern needlework was a constant influence on Western embroiderers. In the nineteenth century appliquéd prayer carpets were exported to Europe. A Persian example, from Resht, at the Victoria and Albert Museum has a red and blue background with applied work in wool outlined with couched cords. There is additional embroidery in chain and satin stitches in yellow and gray silk. The design, with its vase of flowers and birds, bordered by scrolling foliage, although more elaborate, is not unlike the designs of some American appliqué.

As we have seen, the early settlers could not afford to use their precious cloth for frivolous purposes. An appliquéd quilt requires not only a large new piece of cloth for the background, but additional fabric for motifs. Not surprisingly, such quilts did not appear in the colonies in substantial numbers until the mid-eighteenth century, when many fabrics were available: gingham from Scot-

English Rose.

Double Peony and Wild Rose.

Sadie's Choice Rose.

Pomegranate.

Ohio Rose.

Spice Pink.

land, chintz from India, and calico printed in England. Homespun was used for the ground. If trapunto effects were to be used in the quilting, a loosely woven backing was made.

Brides' quilts, with hearts identifying them as nuptial covers, usually were appliquéd. A traditional design for brides' quilts was Rose of Sharon, in one or another of its various forms, possibly inspired by the Song of Solomon. Sometimes, it is said, the prospective husband designed the quilt that the bride-elect was to make.

Friendship and album quilts generally are more sentimental than artistic. As a rule, these are the least impressive of American quilts. It is not difficult to understand why. Each block was designed by a different person, as an act of friendship. Some were signed, giving rise to the group called autograph quilts. It must have been a demanding chore, in tact as well as taste, to arrange the blocks, so varied in pattern and technical skill, into a satisfactory composition. What small frustrations and jealousies must have been aroused as the blocks for the center of the cover were chosen!

Album quilts frequently were given to minister's wives. The blocks were made by members of the congregation and included uplifting quotations and verses from Scripture in addition to the usual signatures. The presentation was made at the minister's home or, if he was a circuit rider, at the home of a devout member of the congregation. Presumably the conversation at such affairs was centered on religious matters. Predestination and free will can be tongue-loosening topics.

One philosophic quilter quoted by George Francis Dow in "The Patchwork Quilt and Some Other Quilts" saw a parallel to these theological questions in quilt making, noting that for piecing, "you just take what happens to come. And that's like predestination," while in appliqué, "Lord sends us the pieces, but we cut them out and put them together to suit ourselves . . . and there's a heap more in the cuttin' out and sewin' than there is in the caliker."

Freedom quilts were made by girls for young men in celebration of their twenty-first birthday. The coming of age was important to a young man; after that his parents or guardian could no longer take his wages, apprentice him, or legally restrict him. Freedom quilts were made before 1825; later, young men were not bound so closely, and the coming of age was not so meaningful.

Many patterns for appliquéd quilts are named. Usually the names were suggested by sights and events close at hand: sun, flowers, animals, occupations, recreations, political and religious convictions, and geographic locations. During Victorian times the

Quilt made by the ladies of the United Presbyterian Church in West Alexander, Pennsylvania, for their pastor, the Rev. Mr. Chauncey Murch, in 1857. Sixteen appliquéd blocks alternate with intricately quilted squares. Art Institute of Chicago, gift of Mr. Frank D. Loomis.

Oak Leaf and Reel.

Martha Washington's Wreath.

Rose of Sharon.

Rose of Sharon.

Rose of Sharon.

Quilt (detail). Appliquéd cotton. Baltimore. Abby Aldrich Rockefeller Folk Art Collection, Colonial Williamsburg. Photograph by the author.

Quilt (detail). Appliquéd printed, plain, and shaded cotton, with embroidered details. Baltimore, ca. 1850. Abby Aldrich Rockefeller Folk Art Collection, Colonial Williamsburg. Photograph by the author.

Baltimore-style album quilt of
appliquéd printed and plain cottons
with details in India ink. 1845–50
(see detail in Plate 19).
Metropolitan Museum of Art,
Sansbury-Mills Fund, 1974.

270 Amish silk bridal coverlet. Pieced
blocks alternate with squares
quilted in Feather Ring pattern.
Ohio, ca. 1870–80. Metropolitan
Museum of Art, purchase, 1974,
Virginia Groomes in memory of
Mary W. Groomes.

Pieced and embroidered silk
coverlet, 1884. Art Institute of
Chicago, gift of Dr. and Mrs.
Ralph W. Graham.

floral wreath and basket of flowers were immensely popular themes. Exceptionally fine examples came from the Baltimore area.

Crazy Quilts

In the nineteenth century a new type of coverlet evolved from the early, randomly patched woolen bedcover. Vaguely similar in form, it was entirely different in function. What began as a thrifty use of scarce material became a purely ornamental and quite costly article of decoration. The silk crazy quilt, often a lap robe, was a sumptuous, but still rather homey, item, perfectly reflecting nineteenth-century America.

Shops offered silk fabrics in a variety of weaves: velvet, damask, and taffeta, watered and brocaded. Developments in chemical dyestuffs encouraged the manufacture of a dazzling array of colors not approached today. Manganese brown became available in 1825, setting off a fad for brown cottons and silks. A single-dye, washfast green, had eluded dyemakers until 1810, when, following a heated competition, a chemist at the Oberkampf establishment in Jouy, France, finally produced one. Green was finally widely marketed in the 1850s. About this time the aniline dyes began to appear, first in aniline mauve, which was received with astounding enthusiasm. Browns and violets, along with alizarin crimsons and black, provided the basic color scheme for the silk crazy quilt, which usually was enlivened by embroidery in gold-colored or multicolored silk. The detail in Plate 22 shows how rich in color these quilts could be.

Special ribbons, laces, preembroidered and painted pieces of fabric, and other materials were produced especially for making crazy quilts. Endless hours were spent painting or embroidering designs of flowers, birds, butterflies, Kate Greenaway figures, patriotic symbols, and other motifs onto some of the larger quilt patches. Most of the coverlets were made by sewing the silks to a backing block a foot or more square. The seams were elaborately embroidered in a great many variations of feather, herringbone, and other stitches in plied silk thread. Then the blocks were set together, the seams embroidered, and a border attached. Bound scallops, lace, or plain black satin or velvet might be used for the border.

Eccentric examples seem to attract the most attention. At the Missouri Historical Society there is a quilt made with fur pieces, feet still attached. Other quilts were sentimental, made from the remnants of the clothing of a well-known person, or with patches and insignia that were souvenirs of some special event.

Detail of appliquéd wool table cover in the Abby Aldrich Rockefeller Folk Art Collection. Colonial Williamsburg. Photograph by the author.

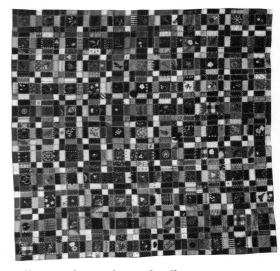

Silk pieced coverlet with silk embroidery and appliqué. Helen Louise Allen Textile Collection, University of Wisconsin.

Honu Ipu (Turtle's Back).

Hawaiian Quilts

Quilts have been made on the Hawaiian Islands for about one hundred and fifty years, the art having been introduced by New England missionary women. These ladies held their first sewing circle aboard the brig *Thaddeus*, on April 3, 1820, as it rode at anchor off the Sandwich Islands. The circle consisted of seven American wives and four distinguished Hawaiian women: King Liholiho's mother, Kalakua; Namahana, also the widow of Kamehameha, father of the king, and Kalakua's sister; and two wives of Chief Kalanimoku, as Stella Jones relates in *Hawaiian Quilts*. The American women, and others who came later, taught Hawaiian girls to spin, card, weave, and sew, and in ten years there were some very competent Hawaiian seamstresses.

Apparently the Hawaiians liked New England quilts. In 1830 Kaahumanu, another royal personage, was given a friendship quilt made in Boston at Miss Dewey's school, and it delighted her. Hawaiian women and girls began to make quilts as complimentary gifts.

The Hawaiian designs were very different from those of the patched quilts of New England. They more nearly resembled the appliquéd quilts made in the South and Middle West after the 1840s. In common with large star patchwork quilts, the composition almost always features one great symmetrical design in the center, but Hawaiian designs are silhouettes, made by women who were accustomed to the stamped designs of their tapas.

There is a story that the typical Hawaiian quilt design originated in 1858, when a son was born to Kamehameha IV and Queen Emma. Island women presented the prince of Hawaii with many quilts on his first birthday. Others say that the form developed at Miss Ogden and Miss Brown's school on Maui. Another legend has it that a woman put out a piece of sheeting to bleach. In the afternoon she saw the shadow of a lehua tree cast against it and cut out this pattern. There are other versions of the shadow theory, as well. Some say the tree was a breadfruit.

Hawaiian women had no bags of scraps left over from dressmaking. Their traditional garments were made of materials felted to size. Instead of piecing together many tiny bits of fabric, they bought new sheets and large pieces of cloth to make their quilts. At first, most were of Turkey red or other strong, bright shades against white backgrounds. Later, scarlet on gold color and other color schemes were added. Calico prints on white or white on calico were other choices.

Ka ua Kani Lehua (The Rain that
Rustles Lehua Blossoms), made for
a member of the Brickwood family
before 1900. Hawaii, late nineteenth
century. Honolulu Academy of Arts,
gift of Damon Giffard, 1959.

Lei Mamo (Mamo Lei), appliquéd quilt made for a member of the Brickwood family before 1900, was owned by the grandmother of the donor. Hawaii, late nineteenth century. Honolulu Academy of Arts, gift of Damon Giffard, 1959.

The Hawaiian crown, coat of arms, and the kahili, the sovereign's feather-tipped staff, appear in many quilts. The patterns shown here include elements adapted from a number of traditional examples. Triangular detail drawings show how these four-way symmetrical appliqué designs may be cut directly from folded cloth, or from paper to make a pattern. With slight variations in cutting, endless versions are possible.

The pineapple is another popular quilt theme.

The fabric was washed to preshrink it and to remove excess dye. The usual quilt was square, to accommodate a design that was symmetrical four ways. The piece of cloth from which the design was to be cut was folded into eighths. Sometimes a single large pattern was cut through the layers, much as paper snowflakes are cut by children, but at other times a separate border design was cut. Some of the borders are continuous, some broken.

Particularly daring designers cut their motifs freehand. Others made a pattern first in paper or tapa. After the design had been cut out and unfolded, it was basted (*pa'i*) to the background fabric (*kahua*). Edges were turned under, and tiny overcasting stitches (*hum u wili* or *kawili*) fixed the layers together. The quilts were assembled on frames made of two-by-fours placed on sawhorses. The frames were often set quite low because the quilters preferred to sit on the ground, rather than on chairs, as they worked.

For the padding, wool was cleaned, bleached, carded, brushed into sheets, and laid evenly over the lining (*pili*), which was stretched on the frame. The top was then laid over the wool, the layers were basted into place, and quilting proceeded in the traditional way, working outward from the center of the quilt. In later quilts commercial batting replaced the home-processed wool.

At first Hawaiians gathered their friends together for quilting bees, as mainland women did. Later quilters achieved more regularity in their stitching by working individually.

The earliest Hawaiian quilting resembles the simplest New England quilting—small squares or parallel lines were worked without regard for the form of the appliquéd design. In addition there were squares within squares, diamonds within diamonds, various plaid patterns, and a version of the shell design. Another pattern, indigenous to one area, was called Honu Ipu (Turtle's Back).

Eventually, the typically Hawaiian contour quilting developed. In this essentially simple method, parallel lines follow the contours of the motifs, accentuating the pattern and enriching the texture of the cover. The most luxurious texture was achieved with woolen padding. The *kulipuu*, or lump hill, is softer and deeper on these quilts.

As on the mainland, women gave admired patterns to friends, but in Hawaii patterns were kept secret more often. Each woman named the patterns she created. Even if a friend altered the design a little, the name of the pattern was not changed. Naturally, patterns (*laus*) were stolen, so women quilted alone, keeping their designs secret until the quilt was finished. They then had undisputed claim to the design. It is said that if a woman saw that someone had pilfered her design, she retaliated with a song composed to embarrass the thief.

As on the mainland, popular designs were wreaths with flowers and birds, historical themes, and occupations. Phenomena of nature were extolled: mountains and craters, rain and mists, streams and waterfalls. *Na Molokama* was a pattern based on the waterfall at Hanalei Bay. Patterns came from a new crystal chandelier at the palace, or the stained-glass windows of a parlor car. Symbols, both obvious and unexplained, were used. Autobiographical designs were worked out, as were religious and patriotic messages (see Plate 18). But the most prevalent designs were trees, birds, and flowers. Grapevines, hibiscus, figs, ferns, breadfruit, pineapples, ohelo berries, and fuchsia were used.

Many quilts were dedicated to Queen Liliuokalani, the last reigning queen of Hawaii, during the detention that preceded her abdication in 1895. Some of her friends went with her into voluntary exile in the palace, where they whiled away the long hours making a silk patchwork quilt. After the annexation of the islands to the United States, public display of the Hawaiian flag was considered treasonable, so many Hawaiians preserved this beloved emblem, along with the coat of arms, in the designs of quilts.

Notes on technique

The old methods for making quilts remain practical today. Templates for patchwork or appliquéd pieces should be cut out of bristol board or stiff paper that will withstand much use. (Old templates were made from a variety of materials: cardboard, old letters, tin, brass, copper, pewter, silver, oak, bone, and ivory.) Make the template in the exact size of the pattern segment, without seam allowances. On the wrong side of the fabric, trace along the edges of the template. As the pieces are cut, add seam allowances of about ³⁄₁₆ or ¼ inch, keeping them uniform in width. The intricacy of the pattern, the size of the pieces, and the weave of the cloth will determine what is a practical seam allowance.

Join patchwork pieces with running stitches on the wrong side of the fabric, frequently checking the pencil lines on both pieces to see that they meet properly.

Some museum quilts still have paper templates (made from old letters) basted in place. The stiff paper helped to keep shapes crisp as the cloth pieces were overcast together on the back. To follow this practice, pin a paper template (brown wrapping paper will do) on the back of each piece, carefully lining up the edges with the penciled seam lines. Pin it firmly in place. Baste the seam al-

Diagram showing the principle of contour quilting.

The coat of arms and crown are often the centerpiece in flag quilts.

Ku'u Hae Aloha (My Beloved Flag) pattern. There are many versions of the central motif.

278

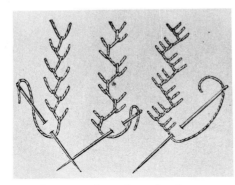

Cat, brier, and coral stitch, three simple variations of feather stitch used for decorating quilt seams, as they appeared in the January 1902 issue of *Home Needlework Magazine*.

lowance down over it. Overcast the seams with stitches, picking up only the cloth. Keep basting and papers in place until the section or block is completed.

An average quilt is 90 inches long, but width and length depend, of course, on the size of the bed. Measure the top surface and the height of the bed. Add a sufficient number of inches for the overhang at the bottom and sides, or to tuck under the mattress if that is how the quilt will be used. A coverlet to be used with a bed-skirt obviously will require fewer inches than a quilt meant to hang to the floor.

Estimates for yardage for any repeat design can be made after the amount of material needed for a single block is determined. Lay out all the pieces for one block and multiply the amount of material required of each color by the number of blocks there will be in the quilt.

For appliqué, pattern pieces may be drawn or traced on the right side of the fabric. To be sure that pencil lines will not show on the finished work, draw the pieces a little "full" so that the line can be turned under as the appliqués are hemmed. In cutting, add ⅛ to ¼ inch all around as a hem allowance. Clip curved edges as you turn them under. As the work proceeds, press appliqué pieces *after* they are stitched down. In pressing patchwork take care not to stretch the seams.

Traditionally the runners and stretchers of most quilting frames were made of four 1-by-2-inch or 1-by-4-inch wooden bars cut 10 to 12 feet long. A flange of ticking to which the layers of the quilt could be pinned or basted was attached along one side of each bar. Holes were drilled at intervals at the ends of the bars so that the size of the frame could be altered by pegging the boards different distances apart. Some frames were adjusted with clamps instead.

Often the frames were set up on four "quilting chairs"—any four low-backed chairs of matching height—or they might be placed on sawhorses. Stress marks along the top of an old chair may indicate that it once was used as a quilting chair.

Two opposite edges of the quilt backing were pinned to the ticking attached to opposite members of the frame. The other two boards were laid under these to form a rectangle and pegged or clamped in place. The two remaining edges of the backing then were pinned in place, the cloth pulled evenly and readjusted where necessary. Then the boards were carefully unfastened, the fabric pulled taut, and the boards secured into position for quilting.

Quilt monogram. Background flower arrangements are slightly altered to fit each letter. The design is adapted from the original in the Art Institute of Chicago.

Crazy quilt (detail) of pieced silk, taffeta, and velvet, with embroidered and painted floral designs and figures worked in outline stitch. Ca. 1880. Art Institute of Chicago, gift of Mrs. Charles I. Seminger.

Kate Greenaway–style figures for outline work from the November 1889 issue of *The Modern Priscilla*. Such figures are often found on crazy-quilt blocks.

280

Detail of a silk crazy quilt adapted from an unusual example in the collection of the Art Institute of Chicago. It includes many painted or silk-embroidered motifs found on nineteenth-century silk quilts.

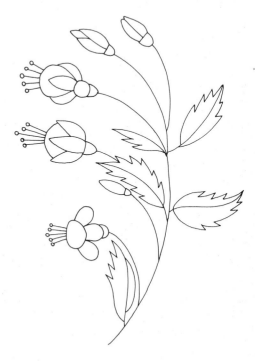

Backings were made larger than the quilt tops so that if the top "grew" in the quilting process, there still would be enough lining to accommodate it. As work progressed, finished parts were rolled onto the frame, which was then readjusted to make the unworked areas more accessible.

Wadding or batting was laid in an even layer over the backing. If sheets of cotton fiber were used, these were overlapped about ½ inch so that thin spots might not develop later. Frequently more than one layer of wadding was used. To keep the filling as even as possible, the layers were placed running in opposite directions.

In an ordinary quilt ½ pound of wool or cotton wadding was used per square yard of quilt. If the wadding was very thick, the layers might be tied rather than quilted. In making tied bedcovers the top was first laid over the filling and basted into place. Usually, but not always, the knotting followed the pattern of the quilt top.

Quilting patterns could either be drawn onto the full area of the coverlet top before it was in place on the frame, or applied little by little as stitching proceeded and the quilt was rolled up on the frame.

The earliest designs sometimes were pounced on with a spur, but tracing wheels were more usual. Designs were also drawn freehand in pencil, chalk, or charcoal. Later, purchased stamped patterns were pounced with a wheel and the design was powdered onto the cloth. Stencils made of mill net, a mesh material charged with glue or starch, also were available. Occasionally a chalk line was used.

Traditional American quilting is usually done in running stitch with one hand held under the frame and the other hand above it. Several stitches are made before the thread is pulled through.

Quilt making has its own jargon. Finished blocks are "set together." To "put in" means to fasten the quilt in its frame. Terms describing progress are: "I've got the set started," "It's put in," "I'm on the second roll," and "I'm almost ready to take out."